I0766538

First Published 2021

© Sarah Ashley 2021

All rights reserved.
No reproduction permitted without the prior consent of the author.

Printed By:-
www.lulu.com

ISBN 978 1 716 26074 2

Introduction

This blog covers the period 22nd April 2019 to 7th April 2020.

Neil Peart, renowned drummer of *Rush*, died on the 7th January 2020. So I used to use his solos as a convenient time to go to the merch desk…

For 11 months I was wittering on about Brexit and planning holidays, gigs and other adventures. Oh how the world has changed! My first post about Coronavirus was on the 7th March. Lockdown followed on the 23rd March.

I can't remember the old normal so this introduction is about the new normal.

From a personal perspective, lockdown was ok. Damien and I could wfh. We had savings due to not commuting or socialising. I enjoyed the peace and quiet. We have a garden. Steve was furloughed, he slept a lot and then kept himself occupied tinkering with his car. The only grief was Kirsten not doing her online school work. She played a lot of Xbox and dyed her hair.

As lockdown gradually eased I had some lovely days kayaking at various points of The Thames and The Medway. Just before Steve's furlough ended we also went to Symonds Yat on the River Wye. That was a great couple of days.

I'm back at the office most days now. Kirsten is back at school. Damien is not going back to the office until March 2021 at the earliest.

Face masks are worn on public transport and in shops. They are causing environmental issues. Economy wrecked. All for 41,902 deaths (to date).

I can't see myself ever going to a gig, festival or travelling abroad again.

Sarah Ashley

24th September 2020

Premenstrual Dysphoric Disorder (PMDD)

On the 14th February 2020 I had an operation that changed my life.

I started my periods at primary school when I was 10. Apart from an embarrassing incident in gymnastics once, they weren't much of an issue.

They were an inconvenience in my teenage years because I spent so much time kayaking, sailing and socialising.

I only recall getting cramps in my late teens. I think I got the best Secret Santa gift at work when I was 18, a hot water bottle. My Secret Santa knew what I went through each month. Still not really any different to an average woman's period. A normal flow, start light, heavy, normal, light – 5 days.

At 19, when I was probably most sexually active with my boyfriend at the time, there seemed to be a correlation between an increased libido and coming on. The good times.

I started getting a headache (wouldn't even register as one nowadays) before I came on after turning 20. My boss at the time called me in about my sickness levels and brought the pattern to my attention, pointing it out what he thought it might be. It was the first time I made a connection to the headaches and my periods. Also the cramps stopped. It was noticeable for the rest of my periods, if I didn't get a headache/migraine, I would get cramps. Such respite the months it was just cramps!

I had a normal enough pregnancy with a ventouse delivery.

I was a nervous first time Mum, worried about being judged. I was also quite lonely. I remember my first incident of throwing a telephone at a wall in a rage. I don't know if I was due on. I asked my Dr for anti depressants and was prescribed fluoxetine. I don't think they did anything. Not sure how long I was on them on that stint. Have been off and on them over the years as that is the only thing Drs will do when you say you have PMT.

My relationship broke down for other reasons. I went to University. In those 3 years, mid to late 20s, the headaches increased in severity and length. Light and sound was painful and movement such as being in a car was guaranteed to cause nausea. Conveniently in the 2nd year, migraine day fell on a subject/lecturer I didn't particularly like. A fellow mature student who was my friend would help with childcare when I had a migraine.

By this time it was obvious I got a headache/migraine before I came on. But I tried avoiding things like cheese and aspartame and caffeine to see if they were causes. No, just the menstrual cycle.

I started taking *Migraleve*. Yellow and Pink tablets, one of which you took at the first symptoms. They worked for a while. I then added ibuprofen at same time. Would mix n match in my mind to stop me becoming immune to one sort but really same active ingredient. I was taking more each month.

I moved in with my new partner. Now each month PMT was getting noticeable. I am now in my early 30s. We decided to go to the Drs about my migraines. I was told I had an attitude problem by one. Another referred me to a neurologist. The neurologist asked me to keep a food and tablet diary for 3 months. I did (plus included mood and part of cycle). Went back and all he said was, 'If it was anything serious you'd be dead by now' and never heard from him again, so I was presumably discharged.

Now I am irritable for a few days before period though I don't think I am. Sometimes minor incidents or indeed nothing at all can trigger a foul mouthed tirade at the top of my voice. In public too. It's either totally out of your control or you feel like you are watching someone else do it and it's still out of your control. Lo betide the person that dares to say 'calm down'…

After the tension comes the migraine. Gets to the stage where either the pain or the painkillers would knock me out. As soon as I come on the migraine goes and you feel like a different person. Period is now very light and only for 3 days.

On a couple of occasions, pans were thrown. On many occasions phones was thrown.

You write it on the calendar as a warning but then you wonder if it's a self fulfilling prophecy or it's used against you when you are trying to validly moan about something. Or at least you tell yourself it's a valid reason.

But still so far, not much different to millions of women. A lot of women suffer with PMT.

I had my daughter when I was 35. It was the best 9 months I'd had for 10 years as I didn't have a single headache. It was a forceps delivery. I was very comfortable being Mum second time round.

The day after I gave birth I got a migraine.

I pretty much had a headache until I stopped bleeding.

For contraception I went to get a Morena Coil fitted. This was the worst. I pretty much had a headache until I got it taken out 6 weeks later.

I am now in my late 30s. The PMT is regular but the migraines are all over the place. They can be before, during, after or a combination or all of them. The main pattern seems to be two a month with the other mid cycle. The Drs prescribe *Maxalt Melt*. This seems to work if taken at exactly the right time.

I'm now in employment where if I can say 'I'm being *me*', I can work from home. Doesn't stop a couple of rages in the office. I don't actually know if they were related to PMT or if I'm just an angry person. I do know I was the person to go to in the office for painkillers. Sometimes I felt a headache coming, would take tablets and go lie down in the car for a couple of hours. I don't really have a sickness record that reflects the amount of headaches I had because of that or maybe it's because they were more at weekends.

I think that by now I am suffering more than most women do with PMT. I start referring to it as "*Extreme PMT*".

It's about to get worse. I knew now that the only solution to my migraines was to have a hysterectomy or something that stopped my periods. I didn't want more children. I certainly didn't want more periods. This could go on for another 15 years or more. All the hours spent in pain, alone, neglecting your family, not having a life.

My 40s were a downward spiral of becoming depressed about headaches, getting headaches, with rages that were getting worse, getting depressed about the rages, feeling guilty about neglecting family and so on and so on. I went to the Drs to try and start the hysterectomy conversation but she just patted me on the knee and said 'I get PMT too dear'.

In this job I generally had 2 days off a month. My managers were great and ignored HR requests about it. The first day would be the migraine. The second day would be migraine 'hangover' where I was dozy from all the *Maxalt Melt* and Ibuprofen I'd taken the day before.

I stopped going to the Drs about my migraines after the final suggestion was trying acupuncture. I just got *Maxalt* on repeat even though I now felt it just delayed the migraine for a day. Useful for going to work on a Friday.

By 45 I was saying I had 2 good days a month where I felt 'normal'. It wasn't that I was crap all month, there was a definite curve related to the cycle about it, just it was only 2 days in that month that where I felt good.

I went to a private migraine clinic. They were thorough in their questions but said not really any experience with migraines and PMT. They could sort migraines out if you were male. They gave a convoluted pill regime to take at different points of the cycle. It was hard to get the GP and this clinic to liaise with the prescription. I tried it out, it was a lot to deal with at the time when you are mental and can't cope. As expected it didn't work. Knew it would be a waste of money. I reiterated to this clinic and my Drs that only a hysterectomy would work. No response from either.

I saw an article on the BBC where a 28 yr old got a hysterectomy due to feeling suicidal during periods. Whilst I was pleased for her, it reiterated that I had been suffering for decades unnecessarily. I contacted Drs again re hysterectomy. They said come in to discuss but when you are mental, you fear and mistrust your own judgement and I was scared it might make migraines worse like the coil did 10 years before. The Drs didn't follow up.

I decided to work in a lower down role but found that more stressful and stopped working for a while. There were other unrelated personal issues for me giving up work. It was at around this time that I noticed a post from my friend on facebook. It said something along the lines of 'A headache for a few hours is PMT, a migraine for six days is PMDD.' Suddenly "*Extreme PMT*" as I liked to call it had a name. By this point I was at my worst. I had depression, anxiety, panic attacks and rages could be at random people in the street for things like not queueing at a bus stop properly. Whilst not suicidal, every morning I would wake up and think 'Shit, I'm still alive'. Suicidal thoughts, leaving family, getting divorced were all regular thoughts during PMT time, I just always thought that a Mother committing suicide would muck up the children more than living with a mental mother which is why that never went further. One day the dustman didn't collect the rubbish and it resulted in a complete breakdown where I couldn't get out of bed for 3 days. I emailed the Drs and all they said was 'We can't assist with rubbish collection'. The email was about my mental state – they didn't comment on that. I always wondered if the many angry crazy emails I sent during this period ever got further than the receptionist.

I seriously began thinking I was either a manic depressive or I was bi-polar. I didn't know how I could get diagnosed.

I stopped buying tickets for gigs and holidays in advance. I was wasting too many by being too ill to go.

So I looked into PMDD some more and did a diary for 3 months of my moods and headaches. I had done this 15 years ago for the neurologist so wasn't surprised at the results.

I also joined a facebook PMDD support group. When I read the posts from other sufferers it was with mixed emotions. Firstly, OMG this is real, these women are experiencing the same as I do. Then, oh no, there are other women experiencing this too. This is awful. The posts made me cry. So many ruined relationships, so many being palmed off by Drs. But mostly their descriptions of the mood swings were articulated so well and captured the hell of it all so much better than I ever can.

I booked a Drs appointment and took my husband just in case they said no. At the ripe old age of 47 I was finally being referred to a gynaecologist. At least 10 years too late.

The gynaecologist had no experience of PMT and didn't seem aware of PMDD. However he took my word for it and gave me a *Zoladex* injection there and then. This was to simulate having a hysterectomy.

OH MY GOD

The next morning I felt like a different person. No depression, no panic attacks, no anxiety, no rages, no pain. I even smiled. That freaked the family out! There was a side effect – hot flushes. Sometimes I would be so drenched I would have to change clothes.

I had 5 further injections over the next 5 months and went back to the gynaecologist. I said there was a 95%+ improvement in my life. He agreed to put me forward for an op (just ovaries n tubes, not hysterectomy). I went for pre op tests and had low iron count. I could not be put on waiting list until iron levels up.

After 6 months of being normal on *Zoladex*, I was petrified of going back to how I was before the injections. They refused because you aren't allowed to have them for more than 6 months. The next period was back to pre injection me, but because of 6 months of no periods, the depression, anxiety and rages seemed worse. I begged for injections to start again at my own risk. They agreed.

It was nice to be normal again for next couple of periods, iron tablets worked, I got on waiting list.

I think I got bumped up the list because of my mental state when not on injections and so I could be recovered in time for a booked holiday.

14th February 2020. Aged 48. Get my ovaries and tubes removed. The gynaecologist (a different one) asked if I wanted HRT. He didn't seem to understand that my body does not want the hormones and that a hot flush was nothing compared to migraines and depression.

The next day I had a headache/migraine. I also had the 'I want divorce/I'm leaving' depression. My worst fears were coming true, having the op had made it worse. I had a week of the usual hell, compounded by thinking this is my life now, there are no solutions.

In hindsight, I think my egg had been released/the hormones were doing their thing before the op as I would have been due on that week.

21st February 2020 onwards – back to normal. No depression or migraines or anything else that has plagued my life for decades. As I had known for DECADES removing my bits was the only solution. Now, 8 months later, I still feel fine. The hot flushes died down quickly but generally still feel too hot most of the time. A minor price to pay for being me again.

I feel let down by the NHS. I feel that they should be more aware of PMDD.

It was nice to tell the support group that it worked. After a while though I turned off the notifications. Selfishly well now, I don't give support. I feel I would just say *Zoladex* and op if *Zoladex* works.

Now I feel well it is hard to describe what it was like. When I wasn't well I wasn't capable of leaving my bed, let alone going to Drs to show them what I was like. So many people have suffered because my Drs didn't understand and didn't act on all of the cries for help. I like to think that I wouldn't have gone through menopause for another 6 years so I had a 7 year reprieve rather than I was cheated of 10 years of my life.

On more than one occasion I have half jokingly said I want to sue the NHS. Not for money but to bring the issue to the attention of Drs. On several occasions I was told how expensive Maxalt Melt are and what I paid for my prescription was a fraction of the price. How much did that cost the NHS (plus didn't work on the mental side of things) v the cost of the operation?

Things are changing. Google it now and lots of things come up.

In May 2019 The World Health Organisation formally recognised PMDD as a gynaecological and mental health disorder in its own right within the International Statistical Classification of Diseases and Related Health Problems, Eleventh Revision (ICD-11)

10

(I am so glad I had the op before lockdown. It was supposed to be in time for Mexico. Lockdown would have been a very different experience for us all if I had been pre op me. Damien commented several times at the start 'I'm so glad you had that operation'. On the flip side, I sometimes think it's sods law that I 'got fixed' and now that I am well enough to go out, we can't.)

Updated Ethnicity Estimates 18ᵗʰ September 2020

Damien

England & Northwestern Europe	74%	>
South East England		>
Surrey & Sussex		
Central Southern England		>
East of England		>
Scotland	19%	>
Norway	5%	>
Wales	2%	>

Think this is more realistic than 100% South East England.

Margaret

England & Northwestern Europe   74% >

    South East England   >

     Surrey & Sussex

   Yorkshire & East Midlands, England   >

     West and South Yorkshire & Derbyshire

   Devon & Cornwall, England   >

Scotland   10% >

Sweden   6% >

Germanic Europe   6% >

Wales   4% >

Sweden appears on Green side still

Donna

England & Northwestern Europe   **63%** >

  South East England >

    Kent

    Surrey & Sussex

  East of England >

    East Suffolk

Germanic Europe   **14%** >

Scotland   **14%** >

Ireland   **5%** >

Sweden   **4%** >

This test new for this book. Has been updated from when test originally done, not sure of changes.

Me

England & Northwestern Europe	66%	>
South East England		>
Surrey & Sussex		
Central Southern England		>
Scotland	32%	>
Wales	2%	>

This has changed a lot. Where has Sweden gone? Why has Scotland increased so much?

Steve

England & Northwestern Europe	**71%**	>
East of England		>
Essex		
South East England		>
Surrey & Sussex		
Scotland	**20%**	>
Wales	**4%**	>
Ireland	**3%**	>
Sweden	**2%**	>

Next test I'm doing is on his Dad, that will be presumably where Ireland and Essex comes from. Assume Sweden is from my Mum and the Green line at present.

Kirsten

England & Northwestern Europe	67%	>
East of England		>
South East England		>
Surrey & Sussex		
Central Southern England		>
Scotland	15%	>
Norway	12%	>
Germanic Europe	3%	>
Sweden	3%	>

Norway from Damien. Sweden and Germanic Europe again assumed from my Mum and the Green line.

Paul

England & Northwestern Europe 57% >

   South East England >

      Surrey & Sussex

Scotland 31% >

Germanic Europe 9% >

Wales 2% >

   Wales >

Sweden 1% >

Quite a mix of Donna and Mum. Scotland seems too high like with me.

Happy Easter
1.   posted 22 Apr 2019, 07:56

Yesterday woke up to the news that churches and hotels had been
bombed in Sri Lanka. At present the death toll is 290. Nobody has
claimed responsibility yet but 24 people have been arrested. Horrific
world we live in.

Jacobina
2.   posted 25 Apr 2019, 12:38

I have no idea who the parents of Alexander Mustart and Christian
Paton are. There is a case for saying Christian's parents were James
Paton and Anne Cowie but only if Christian married Alexander when
she was 15.

If (IF) James and Anne are her parents then she would have a sibling
called Jacobina. I have not come across this name before. Is it just
a feminised version of Jacob or does it have Jacobite connotations?
Jacobina was born in 1764, quite some time after Culloden which was
pretty much the end to the Stuart claim.

And IF they are her parents it didn't really help going back further
apart from one line:-

Henry Cowie (1630 -)
8th great-grandfather
John Cowie (1657 -)
Son of Henry Cowie
Robert Cowie (1698 -)
Son of John Cowie
Anne Cowie (1735 -)
Daughter of Robert Cowie
Christian Paton (1773 -)
Daughter of Anne Cowie

They seem to come from Logie before heading to the Stirling area.

Local

3.   posted 3 May 2019, 18:36

London Boroughs were not involved with this, we vote for councillors at a different time:-

PICTURE

https://www.bbc.co.uk/news/uk-politics-48142181

So it would appear that people were not voting about bins but the Brexit fiasco. If only they had voted like this in the last general election <rolls eyes>

Tenerife

4.   posted 2 Jun 2019, 11:07

So nearly a month since I last did some Ancestry. I've just renewed my membership which seems a waste of money!

A week and a half ago I voted in the pointless European elections. Labour and Conservatives vote was obviously decimated because of the Brexit fiasco. Sadly the voting went as expected:- London was Lib Dem, Scotland was SNP and the rest of the country were Brexit Party. I don't understand. Maybe London and Scotland can become their own countries and stay in the EU. (Obviously what the SNP want!)

Just back from a week in Tenerife, was a great holiday. The resort we stayed in had excellent entertainment in the evening, all covers bands of music I like! Siam Park was a great day out, best waterpark I have ever been too. We also went up a cable car to nearly the top of Tiede mountain, I didn't particularly like the cable car but it was worth it for the amazing views. On the last day we went on a boat trip and saw bottlenose dolphins and pilot whales!

Paton Match

5.   posted 2 Jun 2019, 12:12

Leaving Thrulines for a month has given me some of my own DNA matches to Mustart. Only time to look at one at the moment:-

Predicted relationship: 4th–6th Cousin
Shared DNA: 27 cM across 2 segments

DNA Match
5th cousin
Robert Stewart Wylie (1890 - 1932)
Grandfather of DNA Match
Robert Wylie (1851 - 1923)
Father of Robert Stewart Wylie
Christian Dunn (1823 -)
Mother of Robert Wylie
Janet Mustart (1791 -)
Mother of Christian Dunn
Alexander Mustart (1765 -)
Father of Janet Mustart

I already had to Robert Stewart Wylie - his descendants are new.

Scott Grindlay
6.   posted 2 Jun 2019, 18:27

One of the Mustart public trees has Margaret Moubray Hutchison (2 Sep 1836 Alloa), as marrying a James Scott in 1854 in Alloa.

I think this is incorrect as I have 3 DNA matches on Thrulines with her marrying a Walter Grindlay in 1860 in Dunbarton.

The Alloa marriage location makes more sense and of course I could be connected to these Grindlay matches some other way. Bit undecided as to what to do at the moment. I'll see if the kids n nephew have a Grindlay DNA match too.

Science
7.   posted 2 Jun 2019, 21:20

The Thruline matches have A LOT of primary documentation so I am 100% sure Margaret Moubray Hutchison married Walter Grindlay and have deleted Scott and their family. Have added Walter and there are a lot of hints to go through so there might be some Grindlay stories. I went through all of the other Thrulines and only got one new one where the common ancestor had already been confirmed anyway.

Predicted relationship: 5th–8th Cousin
Shared DNA: 11 cM across 1 segments
and
Predicted relationship: 5th–8th Cousin
Shared DNA: 12 cM across 1 segments

(shared with Predicted relationship: 4th–6th Cousin
Shared DNA: 25 cM across 1 segments relationship not found)
2nd one shared with cousin as well

DNA Match x2
5th cousin
Katherine Sinclair Grindley (1891 - 1977)
Grandmother of DNA Match
Michael Grindley (1866 -)
Father of Katherine Sinclair Grindley
Margaret Moubray Hutchison (1836 -)
Mother of Michael Grindley
Mary Mustart (1797 -)
Mother of Margaret Moubray Hutchison
Alexander Mustart (1765 -)
Father of Mary Mustart

Predicted relationship: 5th–8th Cousin
Shared DNA: 12 cM across 1 segments
shared with same two

DNA Match
5th cousin

Mary Irena Grindley (1903 - 1982)
Grandmother of DNA Match
Michael Grindley (1866 -)
Father of Mary Irena Grindley
Then same as above

Another Jesse Green descendant (via Lucy Green/James Lower)

Parker
8.   posted 2 Jun 2019, 23:26

Samuel Parker (1640 -)
8th great-grandfather
Luke Parker (1672 -)
Son of Samuel Parker
Luke Parker (1714 -)
Son of Luke Parker
Mary Parker (1758 - 1834)
Daughter of Luke Parker
Ann Freer (1784 - 1868)
Daughter of Mary Parker

Gamble
9.   posted 3 Jun 2019, 20:38

This has taken many hours and I can't be bothered to write about it at the moment, two new ancestors confirmed, I only had to Ann Freer previously:-

Predicted relationship: 5th–8th Cousin
Shared DNA: 14 cM across 1 segments

DNA Match
5th cousin 1x removed
Catherine Janet Tookey (1885 -)
Grandmother of DNA Match
Mary Ann Kirby (1858 - 1935)
Mother of Catherine Janet Tookey

Mary Clarke (1820 - 1899)
Mother of Mary Ann Kirby
Mary Freer (1783 -)
Mother of Mary Clarke
William Freer (1750 - 1829)
Father of Mary Freer
Ann Freer (1784 - 1868)
Daughter of William Freer

Predicted relationship: 5th–8th Cousin
Shared DNA: 7 cM across 1 segments

DNA Match
6th cousin 1x removed
Rowlett William Archer (1883 - 1958)
Grandfather of DNA Match
Rowlett Archer (1855 - 1944)
Father of Rowlett William Archer
Thomas Archer (1828 - 1902)
Father of Rowlett Archer
Henry Archer (1779 - 1847)
Father of Thomas Archer
Mary Freer (1752 -)
Mother of Henry Archer
Henry Freer (1719 - 1765)
Father of Mary Freer
William Freer (1750 - 1829)
Son of Henry Freer
Ann Freer (1784 - 1868)
Daughter of William Freer

Henry Freer (1690 -)
7th great-grandfather
Henry Freer (1719 - 1765) Frier/Frere/Freer
Son of Henry Freer
William Freer (1750 - 1829) public trees say William John Freer
Son of Henry Freer

Ann Freer (1784 - 1868)
Daughter of William Freer

Thomas Gamble (1685 -)
7th great-grandfather
Elizabeth Gamble (1719 -)
Daughter of Thomas Gamble
William Freer (1750 - 1829)
Son of Elizabeth Gamble

Ann Freer
10. posted 4 Jun 2019, 18:05

Ann Freer married Timothy Suter in Wakerley, Northamptonshire on the 8th December 1800. Ann and Timothy went on to have at least 9 children. Ann died in Uppingham in 1868.

This I believe has been all I know since writing *'Mum....'* I had a note saying no trace of a baptism. There has been public trees and 'potentials' suggesting her parents were William John Freer and Mary Parker but I don't blindly accept those.

So to get two Freer DNA matches on Thrulines for both William John Freer and his father, Henry Freer was quite exciting. I like science to back up 'potentials'.

It turns out that I was probably looking on familysearch for a birth before 1780 in Northamptonshire which was why I couldn't find a baptism doc. Turns out you need to choose Rutlandshire for Wakerley rather than Northamptonshire and she was born in 1784, making her only 16 when she married.

I still cannot find any evidence her father is called William John. I am just going with William.

The public trees for the DNA matches were a bit of a mess which is why I went through the lines both ways to check that I could get documentation for all of the people, I normally do that after posting the connection but I wasn't happy with the connection until I had done comprehensive checks. Henry Freer was a bit harder to confirm as documents had him as either Frier or Frere, with just one coming up as Freer.

With regards to the public trees confusing me, one just had the name 'K', which I have since established is Mary Ann Kirby but all of the public trees call her Mary Ann Kirby/Tookey/Eales/Ferguson. I will write her up in another post.

Mary Ann Kirby
11. posted 5 Jun 2019, 22:06

Mary Ann Kirby was baptised on the 24th October 1858 at Barrowden, Rutland, one of at least 6 children of James Kirby and Mary Clarke. On the 15th April 1876, aged just 17, she married Samuel Denton in Lanchester, Durham. Later that year she had a daughter, Amelia Elizabeth Denton. I do not have a death doc for Samuel but he must have died c1878.

In 1879, Mary Ann married Robert Tookey in Darlington. Mary Ann and Robert had 3 children before he died c1888. Again no death doc found. A Mary Ann Tookey is listed as a shopkeeper in a Warwickshire trade directory in 1884, I think it unlikely to be her, moving from Durham to Warwickshire.

In 1891, Mary Ann was in service in Woodham, Durham. She is a widow. Her oldest daughter Emma was living with her at her employers residence.

After 1891 it is not clear what happens to her.

Aghhh
12. posted 28 Jun 2019, 20:27

So whilst Boris and Hunt battle it out for Tory leadership, both spouting bollocks about renegotiating the deal even though the EU keeps saying no renegotiation....

EU and Mercosur agree huge trade deal after 20-year talks

> *"The EU and South American economic bloc Mercosur have clinched a huge trade deal after 20 years of negotiations.*
>
> *EU Commission chief Jean-Claude Juncker said it was the EU's biggest deal to date and, at a time of trade tensions between the US and China, showed that "we stand for rules-based trade".*
>
> *Brazil's President Jair Bolsonaro said it was "historic" and "one of the most important trade deals of all time".*
>
> *Mercosur consists of Argentina, Brazil, Uruguay and Paraguay......"*
>
> *https://www.bbc.co.uk/news/world-europe-48807161*

It makes me want to cry. We could have had this. And 20 years. All the Brexiteers saying they will get trade deals. Right in 2040.

Robert Wilson
13. posted 14 Jul 2019, 11:19

Think I've had this one for a while, I don't think I've typed it up before. Sarah Wilson has always been a bit of a dilemma as she was born out of wedlock and her name should be Harris.

Predicted relationship: 5th–8th Cousin
Shared DNA: 10 cM across 1 segments

DNA Match
6th cousin
Eric George Streeton (1913 - 2000)
Grandfather of DNA Match
Martha E Elve (1889 -)
Mother of Eric George Streeton
Alfred Joseph Elvey (1863 -)
Father of Martha E Elve
Joseph Elvey (1831 -)
Father of Alfred Joseph Elvey

Sarah Wilson (1796 -)
Mother of Joseph Elvey
Francis Wilson (1768 -)
Father of Sarah Wilson
John Robert Wilson (1801 - 1886)
Son of Francis Wilson
Sarah Eliza Wilson (1839 - 1925)
Daughter of John Robert Wilson

Smith Steer
14. posted 14 Jul 2019, 12:10

A new confirmation of a nephew line. Samuel Smith has a match.
All of this is new from Jane Smith:-

Predicted relationship: 5th–8th Cousin
Shared DNA: 14 cM across 1 segments

DNA Match
5th cousin of nephew
Beryl Grace Simmons (1925 - 1986)
Grandmother of DNA Match
Frederick Thomas Simmons (1893 -)
Father of Beryl Grace Simmons
Thomas Charles Simmons (1864 -)
Father of Frederick Thomas Simmons
Jane Smith (1842 -)
Mother of Thomas Charles Simmons
Samuel Smith (1807 -)
Father of Jane Smith
Eliza Smith (1831 - 1901)
Daughter of Samuel Smith
John Tucknott (1864 - 1949)
Son of Eliza Smith

Stafford
15. posted 14 Jul 2019, 15:10

Did a couple more nephew Steer ones and then have spent the last couple of hours sorting this out. The DNA match did not have much to go on, no dates or locations, but at least most of it was public.

I cannot get a document connection between Martha Barker and Susan Stafford. The Martha Hunt nee Barker (1863-1945) that I can find is the daughter of John Barker and Mary Lewis. The public trees have her parents as Robert Barker and Harriet English. If that is the case then the next problem is on the 1841 census, Harriet comes up as 18 rather than 10. Then there was an additional spanner in the works with a Susan Stafford 1851 hint giving her husband as John B rather than James.

Anyway, going with science and public trees to get this:-

Predicted relationship: 5th–8th Cousin
Shared DNA: 16 cM across 1 segments

DNA Match of Husband
5th cousin 1x removed
Thomas Hunt (1898 - 1952)
Grandfather of DNA Match
Martha Barker (1863 - 1945)
Mother of Thomas Hunt
Harriet English (1831 - 1908)
Mother of Martha Barker
Susan Stafford (1804 - 1881)
Mother of Harriet English
John Stafford (1775 - 1842)
Father of Susan Stafford
John Stafford (1800 -)
Son of John Stafford
Emma Stafford (1836 -)
Daughter of John Stafford

The new 'evaluate' buttons are rubbish.

Aylen Pitt
16. posted 14 Jul 2019, 15:30

This is husbands first confirmation of the Aylen line:-

Predicted relationship: 5th–8th Cousin
Shared DNA: 15 cM across 1 segments

DNA Match
3rd cousin 1x removed
Aylen
Grandmother of DNA Match
Thomas Arthur Aylen (1883 - 1960)
Father of Aylen
Robert Alfred Aylen (1843 - 1935)
Father of Thomas Arthur Aylen
George Aylen (1869 - 1935)
Son of Robert Alfred Aylen
Annie Louisa Aylen (1891 -)
Daughter of George Aylen

Thomas was in tree, descendants new. The match is not very accurate, he cannot have much Aylen/Pitt in him.

Pratt
17. posted 14 Jul 2019, 15:49

Another new Maddox line confirmation, again with the estimate well off:-

Predicted relationship: 5th–8th Cousin
Shared DNA: 12 cM across 2 segments

DNA Match (1950 -)
3rd cousin 1x removed
Alice Marion Combes (1880 - 1971)
Grandmother of DNA match
Fanny Pratt (1852 - 1937)
Mother of Alice Marion Combes

James Pratt (1815 - 1893)
Father of Fanny Pratt
Edmund Pratt (1854 - 1941)
Son of James Pratt

Had everyone already excluding the match.

Ayling Aylen Ailing Haylen
18. posted 14 Jul 2019, 17:09

Had another Aylen match to Robert Aylen that was a lot easier than the last one. The next Aylen match uses Ayling and Ancestry suggests the match is closer than what the match has for her tree. It depends on what is on the birth cert for 1843 John Ayling but I'm not buying that. He is either a bastard, mother being Eliza or Eliza is his sister and his parents are John and Elizabeth (Betsy) Saunders. On the 1841 census he is listed as their son (Eliza's brother). Adding to complications, his birth doc has Haylen rather than Aylen or Ayling.

Predicted relationship: 5th–8th Cousin
Shared DNA: 7 cM across 2 segments

Option 1
DNA Match
5th cousin 1x removed
Lilian Jean Ayling (1918 -)
Grandmother of DNA Match
Frederick Ayling (1882 -)
Father of Lilian Jean Ayling
John Ayling (1843 -)
Father of Frederick Ayling
John Ayling Aylen Ailing (1801 -)
Father of John Ayling
Thomas Ayling Aylen Ailing (1770 -)
Father of John Ayling Aylen Ailing
Robert Aylen (1815 -)
Son of Thomas Ayling Aylen Ailing

Robert Alfred Aylen (1843 - 1935)
Son of Robert Aylen

Option 2
DNA Match
6th cousin
Lilian Jean Ayling (1918 -)
Grandmother of DNA Match
Frederick Theodore Ayling (1882 - 1939)
Father of Lilian Jean Ayling
John Ayling (1843 - 1922)
Father of Frederick Theodore Ayling
Eliza Ayling (1824 -)
Mother of John Ayling
John Ayling (1801 - 1878)
Father of Eliza Ayling
Thomas Ayling Aylen Ailing (1770 -)
Father of John Ayling
Robert Aylen (1815 -)
Son of Thomas Ayling Aylen Ailing
Robert Alfred Aylen (1843 - 1935)
Son of Robert Aylen
George Aylen (1869 - 1935)
Son of Robert Alfred Aylen

Main
19. posted 14 Jul 2019, 17:40

Husband has a couple of new 5th Gt Grandparents:- John Saunders and Sarah Main.

John Saunders married Sarah Main in Chelmsford in 1795. John and Sarah had at least 7 children between 1797 and 1812.

One of their daughters, Elizabeth, married John Ayling/Aylen c1822 (no doc found yet) and another daughter, Lucy Saunders, married Robert Aylen/Ayling in Orsett, Essex in 1838. Robert being the brother of John of course.

William Tee
20. posted 14 Jul 2019, 18:41

Confirmed back another generation for the boy:-

Predicted relationship: 5th–8th Cousin
Shared DNA: 15 cM across 1 segments

DNA Match
4th cousin 1x removed of son
Rose Batley (1913 -)
Grandmother of DNA Match
Lucy Jane Tee (1880 - 1956)
Mother of Rose Batley
Thomas James Tee (1836 - 1897)
Father of Lucy Jane Tee
William Tee (1797 - 1860)
Father of Thomas James Tee
William Tee (1830 - 1905)
Son of William Tee
Jessie Tee (1868 -)
Daughter of William Tee
William Thomas Gardner (1897 -)
Son of Jessie Tee

Had Lucy, but didn't have Rose as she was born after 1911 census.

Goodman Roots
21. posted 14 Jul 2019, 18:57

First time this line has been verified. Again, had all up to 1911 census already.

Predicted relationship: 5th–8th Cousin
Shared DNA: 8 cM across 1 segments

DNA Match (1940 -)
4th cousin 1x removed of son

Albert Gibbons (1884 - 1960)
Grandfather of DNA Match
Elizabeth Sarah Harrington (1860 -)
Mother of Albert Gibbons
Charlotte Goodman (1831 -)
Mother of Elizabeth Sarah Harrington
James Goodman (1800 - 1854)
Father of Charlotte Goodman
John Goodman (1834 - 1884)
Son of James Goodman
Charles Ernest Goodman (1862 - 1921)
Son of John Goodman

Mardle Mardal Mardell
22. posted 14 Jul 2019, 19:49

Three new matches that confirm the Mardall and Jeffery lines for the
boy:-

Predicted relationship: 5th–8th Cousin
Shared DNA: 15 cM across 1 segments

DNA Match
5th cousin of son
William James Hayes (1918 -)
Grandfather of DNA Match
William James Hayes (1895 -)
Father of William James Hayes
James Hayes (1869 -)
Father of William James Hayes
Jane Mardell (1825 - 1890)
Mother of James Hayes
William Mardal (1791 -)
Father of Jane Mardell
Rose Mardell (1825 -)
Daughter of William Mardal
William Clark (1858 -)
Son of Rose Mardell

Predicted relationship: 4th–6th Cousin
Shared DNA: 21 cM across 1 segments

DNA Match
3rd cousin 2x removed of son
John Towers (1873 -)
Grandfather of DNA Match
Ann Mardle (1828 -)
Mother of John Towers
William Mardal (1791 -)
Father of Ann Mardle
Rose Mardell (1825 -)
Daughter of William Mardal

Predicted relationship: 5th–8th Cousin
Shared DNA: 6 cM across 1 segments
This one private but two lines will do.

That is all of the new common ancestor hints done for husband, nephew, son and myself or at least the match has been assigned to a group. (If I have loads for a particular ancestor, I don't add the match to my tree anymore, I just mark it)

Another Grindlay
23. posted 14 Jul 2019, 21:40

Final Mustart/Paton match (for now) added to tree. I will probably stop writing them up at some point but I still love getting these confirmations after all of these years.

Predicted relationship: 4th–6th Cousin
Shared DNA: 25 cM across 1 segments

DNA Match
5th cousin
Josephine Jessie Marie Grindley (1896 - 1981)
Grandmother of DNA Match
Jonathan Grindlay (1861 - 1917)
Father of Josephine Jessie Marie Grindley

Margaret Moubray Hutchison (1836 - 1897)
Mother of Jonathan Grindlay
Mary Mustart (1797 -)
Mother of Margaret Moubray Hutchison
Alexander Mustart (1765 -)
Father of Mary Mustart

12 Hours
24. posted 15 Jul 2019, 18:28

Next thing I knew, it was 11.30pm....

Haven't had an ancestry day like that for ages - definitely not this
year. Got a divorce to write up but need to get on with life stuff like
the washing up first.

McLaughlin Naismith
25. posted 15 Jul 2019, 20:49

Josephine Jessie Marie Grindley was born in Massachusetts on the
28th August 1896, probably in Holliston, Middlesex as that is where
the family is living in the 1900 census.

By 1910 the family had moved to Lincoln, Providence, Rhode Island.
On the 2nd April 1914, aged just 17, Josephine married David
Naismith. Josephine and David lived with her mother, Catherine
Beston. They had at least two children by 1920.

Lilian McLaughlin was born in Rhode Island on the 21st April 1893.
She married Harold Locke c 1914 and they had at least 4 children by
1920.

Then it is assumed that David Naismith and Lilian McLaughlin had
an affair but I have no evidence to back that up. David and Lilian
married c 1925 and went on to have at least 4 children. Lilian died
on the 7th January 1949 and was buried in Cranston, Providence.
David died on the 20th March 1953 and he is also buried in Cranston.

Josephine in the meantime, had married Alfred William Sarnmark c 1924. Maybe it was these two that had the affair? Or both? Josephine seems to have mainly gone by the name Jessie. Josephine and Alfred had at least 4 children too. Some point after 1940, Josephine moved to Connecticut. She died on the 15th March 1981 in Windham. It is not known when Alfred died.

Lot of unanswered questions there, no marriage dates to the second spouses. Did they get married or just pretend? Did they get divorced? No divorce documents found either.

Lura
26. posted 15 Jul 2019, 21:31

Lura Lavinia Grindley. I was quite convinced it was a typo of Laura but it really seems like it is Lura. She also named one of her children Lura.

Jonathan Grindlay
27. posted 15 Jul 2019, 21:51

Jonathan Grindlay was born in Bonhill, Dunbarton on the 24th September 1861. In 1871 he is living with his family in Leith. At the age of 15, he joined the Navy. His period of engagement started on the 24th September 1879 and was supposed to last 10 years. He is described as being 5ft 3 3/4" with brown hair and brown eyes and no distinguishing marks. On the 11th April 1877 (before engagement?) he started on *HMS Lt Warden* and was there for 3 days before being moved to *HMS St Vincent*. St Vincent was a training ship for boys. However on the 8th May 1877, just 27 days later, he was discharged due to being invalided.

More info on St. Vincent:-
https://en.wikipedia.org/wiki/HMS_St_Vincent_(1815)

Jonathan returns to Scotland and lives in lodgings in Logie. He becomes a baker. Jonathan emigrates to America c 1888 and marries Catherine Beston c 1892. In 1900, they were living in Massachusetts but they had moved to Providence, Rhode Island by 1910.

Jonathan and Catherine have at least 3 children. Jonathan works as a baker all his life until he dies c 1917.

World Connect
28. posted 15 Jul 2019, 22:52

I am sure the last time I looked at Roots web it looked like it wasn't a live site anymore.

I clicked on the link on the Welcome page and it took me there fine today. Tree was uploaded 2nd May 2014, so out of date! It only has 8936 entries.

They are updating the site though. Can't log in under old account, couldn't create an account with the same email address so I have a completely new account now. Have uploaded the Gedo's as of today for the Paterson/Green/Gardner/Knibbs/Brain tree and the Maddox tree.

I hope this new site will still enable ahnentafels to be done.

Mark Green
29. posted 16 Jul 2019, 22:13

I had a hint on Mark Green. It was a photo of him in uniform. I messaged the person to see if they had a better version and they emailed me the whole picture which was a family group photo! It had Mark and Hannah with Albert and Florence and their daughter Eileen. As Eileen is a baby the photo can be dated c 1920.

I do not know how this person has this photo along with quite an extensive Green tree as I can't see how we are related. Mark and Hannah are my Gt Grandparents so he really should be a 2nd cousin or similar to have the photo. Glad he did though! Weird to see a photo of my Gt Grandfather for the first time. Trying to see similarities to my Uncles and I think I can if I ignore the moustache. I have had a photo of an older Hannah for many years so interesting to see what she looked like younger. Can't say I can see any family resemblances to her though.

2nd Cousin
30. posted 17 Jul 2019, 21:02

Well I was right about the relationship - just not to whom. When I didn't see Green in his tree I should have thought to look at his wife! So all good, understand why he has the photo now and it also confirms the people are really those people. When you look at photos of dead people you've never met, you always wonder if they really are those people. That was a really bad couple of sentences, how many times can you write really those people?

I didn't have his wife in my tree, had her brother but there is a good 8 years between them so I assumed he was an only child.

Mary Turfitt
31. posted 17 Jul 2019, 21:22

Mary was born c1861 in Barrowby. She married Matthew Arden in 1881 at Bourne. Mary then had at least six children before dying at the young age of 35, presumably in childbirth.

Harris Arnold
32. posted 30 Jul 2019, 15:00

New ancestor confirmation, Mum, Nephew & Daughter don't appear to be a match:-

Boy
Predicted relationship: 5th–8th Cousin
Shared DNA: 13 cM across 2 segments

Me
Predicted relationship: 5th–8th Cousin
Shared DNA: 10 cM across 2 segments

DNA Match

4th cousin 1x removed to me
Lydia Victoria Farrer (1895 - 1965)
Grandmother of DNA Match
Lydia Jane Creed (1867 -)
Mother of Lydia Victoria Farrer
Emma Harris (1840 -)
Mother of Lydia Jane Creed
Thomas Harris (1810 -)
Father of Emma Harris
Edward Harris (1838 - 1898)
Son of Thomas Harris
Sarah Wilson (1858 - 1930)
Daughter of Edward Harris

I had Emma Harris, rest is new. Can't actually make a connection between Emma Harris as I have her marrying a Joseph Creed but hints suggest she became Trindall not Creed. As with any with a missing link - just agreeing with the science.

About a week ago Boris Johnson became Prime Minister, no surprises there which is why it didn't warrant a post of its own. Also I am really trying to ignore this means a No Deal Brexit on 31st October.

Sayer Cross Carley
33. posted 30 Jul 2019, 18:01

Finally went through Mums common ancestors and assigned to groups. In amongst the many many Barber matches have found a few possibly helpful matches. First ones:-

1. Predicted relationship: 5th–8th Cousin to Mum
Shared DNA: 20 cM across 1 segments

DNA Match
5th cousin 1x removed to me
James T Carley (1902 -)
Gt Grandfather of DNA Match
Joseph Carley (1871 - 1929) * - rest new from here

Father of James T Carley
James Carley (1820 - 1917)
Father of Joseph Carley
Stephen Carley (1794 - 1827)
Father of James Carley
James Carley (1770 -)
Father of Stephen Carley
Jesse Carley (1800 - 1875)
Son of James Carley
Mercy Carley (1854 - 1909)
Daughter of Jesse Carley

2. Predicted relationship: 5th–8th Cousin to Mum
Shared DNA: 18 cM across 1 segments

DNA Match
4th cousin 3x removed to me
Alexander Kinch (1864 -)
Grandfather DNA Match
Alexander Kinch (1822 -)
Father of Alexander Kinch
Frances Cross
Mother of Alexander Kinch
Cross (Joseph 1758 tbc)**
Father of Frances Cross
Sarah Cross (1796 - 1879)* - rest new from here
Daughter of Cross (Joseph 1758 tbc)
Mary Pettifer (1816 -)
Daughter of Sarah Cross
Ann Smith (1836 - 1897)
Daughter of Mary Pettifer

3. Also another Kinch from Alexander 1822
Predicted relationship: 5th–8th Cousin to Mum
Shared DNA: 12 cM across 1 segments

5th cousin 2x removed to me

4. Predicted relationship: 5th–8th Cousin to Mum

Shared DNA: 14 cM across 2 segments

DNA Match
6th cousin 1x removed to me
Kenneth C Walker (1920 - 1978)
Grandfather DNA Match
Esther Ann Risley (1883 - 1952)
Mother of Kenneth C Walker
William Risley (1841 -)
Father of Esther Ann Risley
Joseph Risley (1820 -)
Father of William Risley
Charlotte Sayer
Mother of Joseph Risley
Thomas Sayer (tbc & wife Elizabeth Shepherd)
Father of Charlotte Sayer
Elizabeth Sayer (1771 -)* - rest new from here
Daughter of Thomas Sayer
Thomas Sayer Nicholls (1803 - 1853)
Son of Elizabeth Sayer
James Nicholls (1832 - 1872)
Son of Thomas Sayer Nicholls

Suter
34. posted 30 Jul 2019, 19:20

Another Suter generation back confirmed. I did not have Edward Suter and his descendants in my tree. Haven't got a doc connecting him to William either.

Predicted relationship: 5th–8th Cousin to Mum
Shared DNA: 11 cM across 1 segments

DNA Match
5th cousin 1x removed to me
Thomas Raymond Harrison (1876 - 1906)
Grandfather of DNA Match
Elizabeth Suter Towell (1840 - 1901)
Mother of Thomas Raymond Harrison

Esther Suter (1805 - 1884)
Mother of Elizabeth Suter Towell
Edward Suter (1765 - 1840)
Father of Esther Suter
William Suter (1736 - 1819)
Father of Edward Suter
Timothy Suter (1772 - 1851)
Son of William Suter

Sweet FA
35. posted 30 Jul 2019, 20:37

I think this is a confirmation of something. The connection differs in detail. My tree where the Banks are concerned is not accurate, far too many of them with similar names.

Predicted relationship: 5th–8th Cousin to Mum
Shared DNA: 8 cM across 1 segments

DNA Match
6th cousin 1x removed to me
Harry Adams (1884 - 1959)
Grandfather of DNA Match
George Richard Adams (1847 - 1904)
Father of Harry Adams
Storey Adams (1809 - 1882)
Father of George Richard Adams
Cherry Carter (1785 - 1864)
Mother of Storey Adams
Mary Banks (1757 -)
Mother of Cherry Carter
John Banks (1729 -) & Ann Hursel 1728 they have John Banks 1714-1809 and Anne Bristow 1712
Father of Mary Banks
John Banks (1754 - 1854)
Son of John Banks
Elizabeth Banks (1787 - 1866)
Daughter of John Banks

A couple of great names there; Storey and Cherry. Cherry had a daughter called Fanny Adams. I wonder if she was sweet?

Joseph Cross
36. posted 30 Jul 2019, 21:04

Predicted relationship: 5th–8th Cousin to Mum
Shared DNA: 6 cM across 1 segments

DNA Match
5th cousin 2x removed to me
William E G Kinch (1886 -)
Grandfather of DNA Match
William George Kinch (1855 - 1948)
Father of William E G Kinch
George Kinch (1818 - 1891)
Father of William George Kinch
Francis Cross (1781 -)
Mother of George Kinch
Joseph Cross
Father of Francis Cross
Sarah Cross (1796 - 1879)
Daughter of Joseph Cross
Mary Pettifer (1816 -)
Daughter of Sarah Cross
Ann Smith (1836 - 1897)
Daughter of Mary Pettifer

Another Cross confirmation through a different Kinch line. Francis Cross has a baptism doc confirming Joseph. Still have to look at him.

Edmund Carley
37. posted 26 Aug 2019, 17:08

DNA Match to nephew has made me review this chap. I had him marrying Mary Garman but was obviously not convinced as I also had a Sarah as his wife but not completed.

DNA Match

5th cousin to me
Gladys Mary Carley (1898 - 1991)
Grandmother of DNA Match
Henry John Carley (1859 - 1941)
Father of Gladys Mary Carley
Carley
Father of Henry John Carley
Edmund Carley (1802 - 1886)
Father of Carley
James Carley (1770 -)
Father of Edmund Carley

Then after a lot of work decided my Edmund did not marry Mary Garman so disconnected her and their descendants. He now marries Sarah Hamton or Hampton.

Gladys Mary Carley (1898 - 1991)
Grandmother of DNA Match
Henry John Carley (1860 - 1941)
Father of Gladys Mary Carley
William Carley (1830 - 1881)
Father of Henry John Carley
Edmund Carley (1803 - 1847)
Father of William Carley
James Carley (1770 -)
Father of Edmund Carley

Outrage
38. posted 28 Aug 2019, 17:43

Boris Boris Boris. So full of shit. But now doing scary stuff. Parliament to be suspended in September. Obviously so the others can't do a no confidence vote or similar.

Sigh.

John Osborn
39. posted 7 Sep 2019, 14:13

Finally! An Osborn match. I already had a Hubbard match so was pretty sure Osborn would get one at some point. Think all Green lines are verified now. I only had to George, his descendants are new.

Predicted relationship: 4th–6th Cousin to Mum
Shared DNA: 22 cM across 1 segments

DNA Match
4th cousin 1x removed to me
Maria Jane Schmae (1870 -)
Grandmother of DNA Match
Jane Maria Osbon (1845 - 1876)
Mother of Maria Jane Schmae
George Osbon (1820 -)
Father of Jane Maria Osbon
John Osbon (1782 - 1867)
Father of George Osbon
Hannah Lucy Osbon (1818 - 1875)
Daughter of John Osbon
Albert Green (1853 - 1914)
Son of Hannah Lucy Osbon
Mark Green (1875 - 1935)
Son of Albert Green

Lauder Galloway
40. posted 7 Sep 2019, 20:48

Nephew has two new common ancestor hints to Alexander Mustart which appear to be just based on thrulines, one of the matches only has 16 people in her tree.

Predicted relationship: 5th–8th Cousin
Shared DNA: 14 cM across 1 segments

Predicted relationship: 5th–8th Cousin
Shared DNA: 17 cM across 1 segments

The matches are based on William Lauder and his wife Isabella Galloway. Isabella Galloway was born on the 14th May 1806 in

Alyth, Perth. She was the daughter of Andrew Galloway and Rachel Mustard which I assume is Mustart.

Rachel Mustart married Andrew Galloway on the 26th March 1804 in Edinburgh. Rachel was born on the 20th May 1782 and baptised on the 1st June in Tulliallan, Perth. Her parents were Alexander Mustart and Rachel Shaw. (Schaw?)

This is the Alexander Mustart they are matching to me. (nephew) From Tulliallan with a daughter called Rachel, married to a Rachel. However my Alexander Mustart was married to Christian Paton and none of their five children is called Rachel.

This alternate Alexander Mustart had at least 4 children with Rachel Shaw; Isabel 1771, John 1772, Lilly 1776 and Rachel (the thrulines match) 1782. They were all born in Tulliallan. In addition, an Alexander Mustart and Rachel Schaw had two baptisms at Alloa as well, an Alexander in 1783 and a Lilias in 1785.

My Alexander Mustart has a potential ancestor hint that John Mustart and Lilly Taylor were his parents. I stopped at him because there was no trace in Stirlingshire 1740-1770 and too many elsewhere.

However the father of Rachel, Alexander Mustart, was born on the 1st January 1847 and baptised in Culross (Perth/Fife not sure which) on the 8th January. His parents were John Mustart and Lilly Taylor.

I do not believe that the Thrulines hint and the potential ancestor hint are correct. Rachel Mustart is not the sister of my 3rd Gt Grandmother Jean Mustart.

So what is the DNA connection?

Is it possible that my Alexander and Rachel are siblings?

Buist Westwood Bruce Robinson Cowie Kerr
41. posted 7 Sep 2019, 21:20

If Alexander Mustart is the brother of Rachel Mustart, I can possibly go quite far back on a few lines. The only documentation I have for him is the marriage to Christian Paton, there are no baptism docs to match him to Alexander (1747) & Rachel Shaw at all.

John Mustart (1706 -) & Lilly Taylor
6th great-grandfather/6th gt grandmother
Alexander Mustart (1747 -)
Son of John Mustart
Alexander Mustart (1770 -)
Son of Alexander Mustart
Jean Mustart (1792 - 1869)
Daughter of Alexander Mustart
Alexander Paterson (1825 - 1865)
Son of Jean Mustart

Of course John Mustart is a dead end with two options in 1706 in Rattay, Aberdeenshire. Lilly Taylor too common.

So going back on the Shaw line:-

Willie Buist (1573 -)
10th great-grandfather
Euphame Buist (1611 -)
Daughter of Willie Buist
Adame Westwood (1647 -)
Son of Euphame Buist
James Westwood (1687 -)
Son of Adame Westwood
Isabel Westwood (1710 -)
Daughter of James Westwood
Rachel Shaw (1746 -)
Daughter of Isabel Westwood
Alexander Mustart (1770 -)
Son of Rachel Shaw
Jean Mustart (1792 - 1869)
Daughter of Alexander Mustart

James Westwood (1607 -)

9th great-grandfather
Adame Westwood (1647 -)
Son of James Westwood
James Westwood (1687 -)
Son of Adame Westwood

Johne Bruce (1620 -)
9th great-grandfather
Kathrine Bruce (1653 -)
Daughter of Johne Bruce
James Westwood (1687 -)
Son of Kathrine Bruce

Elspet Robinson
9th great-grandmother
Kathrine Bruce (1653 -)
Daughter of Elspet Robinson

John Cowie
8th great-grandfather
Euphain Cowie (1686 -)
Daughter of John Cowie
Isabel Westwood (1710 -)
Daughter of Euphain Cowie

Janet Kerr
8th great-grandmother
Euphain Cowie (1686 -)
Daughter of Janet Kerr

Buist is an unusual name. Loving finally getting a 'real' Scottish name; Bruce. And you can't get more Scottish than Bruce. Of course I doubt there is any connection to The Bruce. Not that I think I want to have one, he wasn't very nice really.

This is all reliant on Rachel Shaw being the mother of Alexander Mustart. I might disconnect it all until I get more evidence.

Sanders Mustard

Search Alexander Mustart 1740-1770 Scotland and 7 possible options come up on Scotland's Birth & Baptisms, 1564-1950 on familysearch.

There are 3 without a first name, there is one called Sanders (which amuses me greatly - should be a sauce at KFC), so that leaves 3 options.

There is the one all the hints go for - John Mustard & Lilly Taylor in 1747 in Culross, making him 41 when he married Christian Paton and 50 when youngest born. Not impossible.

Then there is 1756 in Dundee - parents Alexander Mustard & Jean Bartan. Dundee is too far away to make this likely.

The final one is 1759 in Meigle, father William Mustard. This would make him 29 when he married and 38 when youngest born which is more realistic.

Of course the real one might not be there at all going by my experience with Alexander Paterson.

Nanns Mustard
43. posted 7 Sep 2019, 23:55

Lilias (or Lily) Taylor was the daughter of Thomas Taylor. She was baptised on the 9th December 1716 in Findo-Gask, Perthshire. On the 22nd July 1743, Lilias married John Mustart in Alloa. Back in Perthshire, but now Culross, they had a son, James. He was born on the 10th August 1744 and was baptised in Culross on the 14th. Three years later on the 1st January 1747, they had another son, Alexander. He was baptised in Culross on the 8th. This time Lilias is documented as Lily. Their third child was Ann, born on the 13th August 1751. She was baptised in Culross on the 20th. Lily rather than Lilias again.

Apart from these 3 children, nothing more is known about Lilias Taylor and John Mustart.

As an aside and because I am juvenile, thought I would mention there is a Nanns Mustart baptised on 16th December 1750 in Rattray, Perthshire. Her father is John Mustart. So now I have seen a Nanns Mustard and a Sanders Mustard. I am so unfunny.

Alexander Mustart
44. posted 8 Sep 2019, 00:58

So I have now decided that the hints were correct. Alexander is the son of John and Lilias. Alexander is the father of Rachel not the brother. Should have taken my first instinct that he married twice. None of the public trees have him as marrying twice though apart from one that has a Margaret Donaldson as his first wife. (An Alexander Mustart married a Margaret Donaldson in Culross on the 14th March 1778)

My 4th Great Grandfather, Alexander Mustart was born in Culross on the 1st January 1747. He was the son of John Mustart and Lilias Taylor. He was baptised in Culross on the 8th January 1747. I believe he married Rachel Shaw c1770 but cannot find a document. Alexander and Rachel lived in Tulliallan, Perth and went on to have at least 4 children there. They then moved to Alloa and had another 2 children. Presumably, Rachel dies c1786 in Alloa. On the 24th February 1788, Alexander remarried. His new wife was Christian Paton and they had 5 children, one of which was my 3rd Great Grandmother, Jean Mustart.

So the DNA matches are descendant from Alexander just not Christian, they are half distant cousins. Which means that I haven't got Bruce or all of those other lines in my earlier post as Rachel Shaw is not my blood.

DNA Match
5th cousin *half
Isabella Lauder
Grandmother of DNA Match
George Lauder (1836 -)
Father of Isabella Lauder

Isabella Galloway (1806 -)
Mother of George Lauder
Rachel Mustart (1782 -)
Mother of Isabella Galloway
Alexander Mustart (1747 -)
Father of Rachel Mustart
Jean Mustart (1792 - 1869)
Daughter of Alexander Mustart
Alexander Paterson (1825 - 1865)
Son of Jean Mustart

Perthshire
45. posted 10 Sep 2019, 08:52

Mustart lines come from Rattray, Culross, Alyth, Findo-Gask and Tulliallan. (with some visions 150 years later):-

John Mustart (1706 -) Rattray
5th great-grandfather
Alexander Mustart (1747 -) Culross
Son of John Mustart
Jean Mustart (1792 - 1869)
Daughter of Alexander Mustart
Alexander Paterson (1825 - 1865)
Son of Jean Mustart

"In 1887, John Bartholomew's Gazetteer of the British Isles described Rattray like this:

Rattray.-- town (police burgh) and par., Perthshire - par., 5382 ac., pop. 3051; town and police burgh, on river Ericht, opposite Blairgowrie, pop. 2533; the town comprises the vils. of New Rattray; P.O; and Old Rattray; P.O.; flax and jute spinning is carried on."
 http://www.visionofbritain.org.uk/place/16571

"In 1887, John Bartholomew's Gazetteer of the British Isles described Culross like this:

Culross, parl. and royal burgh, small seaport, and par., in detached part of Perthshire, on N. shore of Firth of Forth, 2½ miles SE. of East Grange sta., this being 6 miles NW. of Dunfermline and 7½ miles SE. of Alloa -- par., 7584 ac., pop. 1130; parl burgh, pop. 373; royal burgh, pop.

380; P.O., T.O.; has mfrs. of linen. There are ruins of a Cistercian abbey founded in 1217. Near the abbey ruins is Culross Abbey House, seat of the Earl of Elgin; also Culross Park. C. unites with Stirling, Inverkeithing, Dunfermline, and Queensferry, in returning 1 member to Parliament. "
http://www.visionofbritain.org.uk/place/16938

John Taylor (1633 -) possibly Doune
8th great-grandfather
Thomas Taylor (1659 -) Fenwick Ayr?
Son of John Taylor
... above 2 not 100%
Thomas Taylor (1680 -) Alyth
6th great-grandfather
Son of Thomas Taylor
Lilias Taylor (1716 -) Findo-Gask
Daughter of Thomas Taylor
Alexander Mustart (1747 -)
Son of Lilias Taylor

"In 1887, John Bartholomew's Gazetteer of the British Isles described Alyth like this:

Alyth, par. and town, partly in Forfarshire but chiefly in Perthshire, 23¼ miles NW. of Dundee by rail, 23,296 ac. (of which 3932 are in Forfarshire), pop. 3321; town, pop. 2377; P.O., T.O., 2 Banks; has mfrs. of woollen and linen goods; jute-spinning is also carried on."
http://www.visionofbritain.org.uk/place/16462

"In 1887, John Bartholomew's Gazetteer of the British Isles described Findo Gask like this:

Findo-Gask, par. and hamlet (ry. sta. Balgowan), Perthshire, --par., 5185 ac., pop. 364; hamlet, 2 miles SE. of sta. and 8 miles SW. of Perth; P.O., called Gask; the par. is traversed by a Roman road."
http://www.visionofbritain.org.uk/place/17064

John Watson (1630 -)
8th great-grandfather
John Watson (1652 -) Alyth
Son of John Watson
Margaret Watson (1689 -) Tulliallan
Daughter of John Watson
Lilias Taylor (1716 -)
Daughter of Margaret Watson

"In 1887, John Bartholomew's Gazetteer of the British Isles described Tulliallan like this:

Tulliallan, par., in detached part of Perthshire, on river Forth, 3586 ac., pop. 2207; contains Kincardine; Tulliallan Castle, seat of Lord William Osborne, is near Kincardine, and 4½ miles SE. of Alloa."
http://www.visionofbritain.org.uk/place/16714

These two not Perth:-

Johnne Scobie (1585 -)
9th great-grandfather
Johne Scobie (1617 -) Edinburgh
Son of Johnne Scobie
Bessie Scobie (1648 -) St Ninians
Daughter of Johne Scobie
Margaret Watson (1689 -)
Daughter of Bessie Scobie

Alison Crawford (1573 -) Alisone Crawfurd/Alisone Crafurd/Alysone Craufuird
9th great-grandmother
Johne Scobie (1617 -)
Son of Alyson Crawford

Silver War Badge
46. posted 15 Sep 2019, 09:48

The Silver War Badge was issued in the United Kingdom and the British Empire to service personnel who had been honourably discharged due to wounds or sickness from military service in World War I.

Suspending Parliament was Unlawful
47. posted 24 Sep 2019, 11:33

That is all. :) :) :)

King n Carley
48. posted 24 Sep 2019, 12:44

Two new ones:-

Predicted relationship: 4th–6th Cousin to daughter
Shared DNA: 20 cM across 1 segments

Predicted relationship: 5th–8th Cousin to me
Shared DNA: 18 cM across 1 segments

DNA Match
4th cousin 1x removed to me
Emily E Bainton 1913-1992 (had to here, her descendants new)
Grandmother of DNA Match
Edgar James Bainton 1886-1970
Father of Emily E Bainton
Emily Hewitt 1855-1933
Mother of Edgar James Bainton
Elizabeth King 1832-1913
Mother of Emily Hewitt
Joseph King 1802-1838
Father of Elizabeth King
John King 1830-1888
Son of Joseph King

No nephew or son match for that one

Next one - everyone except daughter:-

Predicted relationship: 5th–8th Cousin to son
Shared DNA: 6 cM across 1 segments

Predicted relationship: 5th–8th Cousin to nephew
Shared DNA: 7 cM across 1 segments

Predicted relationship: 5th–8th Cousin to me
Shared DNA: 6 cM across 1 segments

Predicted relationship: 5th–8th Cousin to mum
Shared DNA: 12 cM across 2 segments

DNA Match
4th cousin to me
Ruby Wilson 1921-
Grandmother of DNA Match
Rose Lilian Charman 1889- (had to here, can't find descendants
but going with science)
Mother of Ruby Wilson
Ruth Carley 1851-1910
Mother of Rose Lilian Charman
Jesse Carley 1800-1875
Father of Ruth Carley
Mercy Carley 1854-1909
Daughter of Jesse Carley

72
49. posted 24 Sep 2019, 14:30

Had to look into the Carley documents as I don't like gaps and this
is where I am at so far:-

Ernest Charles Osbourne was born on 24 December 1886. He
married Lizzie Hollick and they had six children together. He then
married Ruby Wilson and they had five children together. He died in
October 1964 in Essex at the age of 77.

It does look like he was in his 70s, I reckon 72 when he and Ruby Wilson had the mother of the DNA match. I have messaged the match to see if this is correct.

Snelling
73. posted 24 Sep 2019, 15:11

Just one line unconfirmed now on the Green side and it is quite frustrating not to have the full set. Still no Snelling matches. Mary Shelley being confirmed by her father indicates that John Bloomfield Snelling is right but she equally could have done a naughty..!

Barber n Pell
74. posted 29 Sep 2019, 10:07

Mum had about 5 more Barber matches today. Other 'new' matches were Pell. Have not added any to tree.

Weston Bourne
75. posted 5 Oct 2019, 20:50

Only had Mary Weston. Her parents of Thomas Bourne and possibly Susanna are new. Therefore Henry and his descendants all new too:-

Predicted relationship: 5th–8th Cousin to Mum
Shared DNA: 13 cM across 2 segments

DNA Match
6th cousin 1x removed to me
George Ignatius Bourne 1867-1896
Grandfather of DNA Match
Amos Bourne 1838-1903
Father of George Ignatius Bourne
Henry Bourne 1801-
Father of Amos Bourne
Henry Bourne 1772-
Father of Henry Bourne

Thomas Bourne 1746-
Father of Henry Bourne
Thomas Bourne 1710-
Father of Thomas Bourne
Mary Bourne 1750-1787
Daughter of Thomas Bourne
Mary Weston 1769-
Daughter of Mary Bourne
Jesse Carley 1800-1875
Son of Mary Weston

Lewis Alwork
76. posted 5 Oct 2019, 21:34

Another Green extension confirmed. Had this one for a while but only just added to tree. Amos Lewis descendants are new.

Predicted relationship: 4th–6th Cousin to Mum
Shared DNA: 26 cM across 2 segments

DNA Match
5th cousin 2x removed to me
Percy Thomas L Blackwell 1883-1954
Grandfather of DNA Match
Louisa Martha Lewis 1843-1922
Mother of Percy Thomas L Blackwell
Amos Lewis 1811-1902
Father of Louisa Martha Lewis
William Lewis 1779-1848
Father of Amos Lewis
John Lewis 1729-
Father of William Lewis
Lucy Lewis 1757-
Daughter of John Lewis
John Osbon 1782-1867
Son of Lucy Lewis

Urbane
77. posted 5 Oct 2019, 22:39

Amos Lewis and Sarah Leaver had at least 10 children between 1832 and 1857. One of these was Urbane Richard Lewis. Urbane was born in Willingdon on the 9th January 1853. He lived with his family in Willingdon, working as a bricklayer, until at least 1871. I cannot find him in 1881. Name varies a lot from document to document, other variations are:- Urbane Rd Lewis, Urbane R Lewis, Urbano Seuss, W Bane Lewis and Urbane Lewis. On the 19th October 1884 he married Elizabeth Caroline Taylor. Elizabeth had been previously married and had a daughter, Florence Clara Toomey. Elizabeth and Urbane went on to have at least 4 children. He was still working as a bricklayer in 1911.

On the 16th January 1922, he was admitted to Chatham Workhouse. He was discharged later that year on the 14th October. He was admitted again on the 8th October 1925. Urbane died there on the 16th June 1926.

There is nothing unusual about him apart from his name.

Carly Line 2
78. posted 6 Oct 2019, 10:51

John Cruttenden and Ann are my 7th Gt grandparents. Public trees have her surname as Carly. I thought that was too much of a coincidence so left it.

Today I looked at a hint for Ann. An Anne Carly was baptised in Salehurst on the 21st July 1723. Her parents are Richard Carly and Elizabeth.

Richard & Elizabeth appear to only have 2 children, the other one being Elizabeth, who was baptised in Salehurst in 1725.

My main Carley/Carly line are in Etchingham around this time. Etchingham is under 4 miles away from Salehurst so they probably are connected. Cannot find any Richard Carley/Carly born in Salehurst between 1680 and 1700. Dead end at 8th Gt Grandparents.

Not Long Now
79. posted 12 Oct 2019, 22:50

Got another Stephen Green confirmation for Mum and everyone except daughter had another Timothy Suter confirmation.

I have delayed writing next book until 31st October. Hoping the introduction might have a finalised Brexit result to comment on.

Janet Paterson
80. posted 13 Oct 2019, 00:32

Had what might be a good hint on Janet Paterson. I never knew what happened to her after the 1841 census when she was living in St Ninians with her family, aged 9.

The name Janet Paterson is just too common to search on.

Anyway, this hint has her marrying William Struthers on the 18th November 1850 in St Ninians.

Appendix 9 Revised
81. posted 13 Oct 2019, 08:57

Redone the Paterson tree. Still no further back than Charles Paterson but this includes the Mustart and Paton lines. Did not extend the Taylor line (inc Stuart, Watson, Scobie, Crawford, Lawder as not 100% on those).

PICTURE

William Struthers
82. posted 13 Oct 2019, 09:45

William Struthers was born in Glasgow c1830. On the 18th November 1850, he married Janet Paterson at St Ninians. He worked as a nailer all his life. William and Janet went on to have at least 5 children between 1850 and 1865. Janet is not located after the birth of their daughter, Mannie Fleming Struthers in 1865 so I assume she died in childbirth.

Helen Jaffray was born in Stirlingshire c1842. She married William Fisher on the 10th June 1864 at St Ninians. Helen and William had at least 2 children before William Fisher presumably died.

Helen then must have married William Struthers c1870 but no document is located to confirm this. Helen and William Struthers went on to have at least 7 children between 1871 and 1880.

There are no death docs for Helen or William S but I reckon she died in the 1880s and he died in the 1890s.

I am still not 100% that this is MY Janet Paterson. A search brings up lots of alternate marriages, these are the more obvious choices:-

> Janet Paterson
> Daniel Mcdougall
> 25/05/1851 Saint Ninians,Stirling,Scotland
>
> Janet Graham Paterson
> George Bateman
> 05/01/1851 Saint Ninians,Stirling,Scotland
>
> Janet Paterson
> Archibald Mcinnes
> 25/03/1865 Saint Ninians,Stirling,Scotland

I cannot go any further on their 5 children anyway so it doesn't really matter.

Fifth Lord Gartnafueran
83. posted 13 Oct 2019, 09:54

According to public trees, the father of who I potentially think is my 9th Gt Grandmother, Janet Stuart, is the Fifth Lord Gartnafueran Stuart Alexander (1580-1618). I don't know what Fifth Lord

Gartnafueran means or how to pronounce it but it is probably unlikely.

Tunisia
84. posted 15 Oct 2019, 20:38

Gordon John Wingate was born in 1916 in Steyning. He lived with his family in Brighton until he married Joyce Gwendoline Green in 1942.

In WW2 Gordon was a Guardsman in the Grenadier Guards. His regiment, 2618151, were based in North Africa during the war. He died in Tunisia on the 27 Apr 1943 and was buried at Massicault War Cemetery in, Borj el Amri, Manouba, Tunisia.

Inkerman
85. posted 15 Oct 2019, 22:13

James Inkerman Green was born in Denton on the 3rd April 1855 and was baptised in Newhaven on the 6th May. His parents were John Jarvis Green and Ann King, there is no immediately obvious reason for his middle name.

In 1871 he is on *HMS Martin* as a 'boy 2nd class'. He joined the Royal Navy properly on the 8th December 1872. His service number was 66180.

James first served on the *Immortalite* as an ordinary seaman. Then on the 1st July 1874 he was promoted to able seaman and moved to *Excellent*. James had a couple of months on the *Lively* in 1878 before returning to *Excellent*. On the 13th August 1879 he was promoted to leading seaman and was now serving on the *Minotaur*. The next promotion is hard to read, maybe 2nd lieutenant. This was on the 27th August 1880 on the *Duke of Wellington*. James was also on the *Crocodile* and *Northampton* before becoming (presumably) 1st lieutenant on the 27th February 1881. He was on several other ships, sometimes returning to ones he had served on previously. No idea what the promotion in January 1890 is whilst he was serving on *Orlando*.

James' conduct is routinely described as exemplary or very good. He received good conduct badges on the 1st June 1876, 1st June 1881 and 1st June 1886. He finally left the Navy on the 31st March 1893.

Whilst in the Navy, James joined the Masons. He was initiated into the Landport Lodge in 1883.

James married Alice Scott in Portsea Island in 1884. They don't appear to have had any children whilst he was in the Navy but had at least 3 after. (One of which was James Inkerman George Green, who also became a Lieutenant in the Navy).

In 1895, James ran the North Star Public House in Hampshire and in 1898 he ran the Sea Horse Tavern Public House in Sussex. In the 1901 census his occupation is given as "beer, sailer" . (This is corrected to "beer, pub, sailer").

James died in Hastings on the 20th April 1901, just after that census. He was the beer house keeper at the Black Horse inn in Priory Road, Halton, Hastings at the time. He left £1,421 to Alice.

Elizabeth Green
86. posted 15 Oct 2019, 23:06

John Green married Hannah Buxton in Seaford on the 27th April 1812. They went on to have at least 7 children, one of which was Elizabeth Green. Elizabeth was baptised on the 2nd March 1817 in Seaford. She married Charles Costick in Brighton on the 18th July 1837.

Another Green Costick connection!

Cosstick
87. posted 15 Oct 2019, 23:25

This isn't a new verification, John Green verified before. Why this is unusual is that I already had this match in my tree. This is because I have their Great Nephew already as a match though.

Predicted relationship: 5th–8th Cousin
Shared DNA: 15 cM across 1 segments

DNA Match already in tree
6th cousin 2x removed
Edwin John Cosstick 1856-1929
Grandfather of DNA Match
Edwin Cosstick 1833-
Father of Edwin John Cosstick
John Cosstick 1795-
Father of Edwin Cosstick
Mary Green 1767-1848
Mother of John Cosstick
Henry Green 1736-
Father of Mary Green
John Green 1712-1770
Father of Henry Green

Coastguard
88. posted 16 Oct 2019, 22:31

Charles Costick was born c1808 in Seaford. On the 13th October 1829 he joined the Royal Navy. Charles served on the *Volage* until the 15th January 1833. He was then on the *Racer* until the 20th March 1836. The next ship was *Thunder* until the 4th May 1837.

Charles married Elizabeth Green on the 18th July 1837 at St Nicholas in Brighton. After marrying, his last ship was the *Stork* which he was on until 15th November 1837. Charles then transferred to the coastguard.
This is a snip from https://www.genuki.org.uk/big/Coastguards/C (it saves me typing it up):-

PICTURE
Charles died in 1876 and was buried in Herne on the 14th January 1876.

2nd Deal

89. posted 17 Oct 2019, 22:16

I am a tad gobsmacked. Boris and the EU have agreed on a deal. I couldn't see how Ireland border proposals would keep anyone happy but it's sorted. Now we go back to the farce of our Parliament. It won't be agreed for a variety of reasons. 1) Lib Dems and other remainers don't want to leave 2) Jeremy Corbyn wants a general election or doesn't - who knows? 3) The flaming DUP. And the circle of Brexit hell will forever keep on turning. Part of me wants Boris to go full on Dictator and ignore what Parliament vote for. I am sure the Express, Telegraph & Daily Mail readers really do want that. Of course I want the deal refused, I don't want to leave.

Summary
90. posted 17 Oct 2019, 22:54

"Boris Johnson and EU leaders have hailed the deal they have struck to take the UK out of the bloc on 31 October in an "orderly" fashion.

The prime minister now faces a battle to get the deal through Parliament on Saturday, with the DUP opposing it.

DUP deputy leader Nigel Dodds accused Mr Johnson of being "too eager by far to get a deal at any cost".

European Council President Donald Tusk did not rule out an extension to the Brexit deadline if MPs rejected it.

EU Commission President Jean-Claude Juncker earlier said: "We have a deal so why should we have a prolongation."

But his Brussels colleagues have been more cautious, with Mr Tusk saying he would "consult" the leaders of EU member states about a possible extension if one was requested by the UK.

He said Boris Johnson's acceptance of customs checks at the point of entry into Northern Ireland, which the DUP objects to, had made a deal possible.

Mr Johnson has repeatedly insisted the UK will leave the EU on 31 October and he urged MPs to "come together" and "get this excellent deal over the line".

He added: "Now is the moment for us to get Brexit done and then together work on building our future partnership, which I think can be incredibly positive both for the UK and for the EU."

The EU and UK negotiating teams worked round-the-clock on the legal text of the deal, but it will still need the approval of both the UK and European parliaments.

In a statement, the Democratic Unionist Party, which the government relies on for support in key votes, said: "These proposals are not, in our view, beneficial to the economic well-being of Northern Ireland and they undermine the integrity of the Union.

The DUP deputy leader Nigel Dodds criticised Mr Johnson, telling BBC News: "If he'd held his nerve - and held out - he would, of course, have got better concessions which kept the integrity, both economic and constitutional, of the UK."

He said he expected a "massive vote" against Mr Johnson's deal on Saturday in the House of Commons - and the DUP expected to "play a crucial role" in amending the legislation.

The winning post for votes in the House of Commons is 320 if everyone turns up - seven Sinn Fein MPs don't sit and the Speaker and three deputies don't vote.

There are currently 287 voting Conservative MPs. The prime minister needs to limit any rebellion among them.

Then, if the DUP won't support his deal, he'll need the backing of 23 former Conservative MPs who are currently independents. Most will probably support the deal, but not all.

That's still not quite enough, though, so the PM will also need the backing of some Labour MPs and ex-Labour independents. In March, when MPs voted on Theresa May's deal for the third time, five Labour MPs backed it, plus two ex-Labour independents.

This time it's likely to be a bit higher than that because several MPs have said they would now back a deal.

All this still leaves the vote very close. And it's possible some MPs could abstain, making it even harder to predict the outcome.

Most of the deal is the same as the one agreed by Theresa May last year - the main change is the Northern Ireland proposal.

The UK will continue to abide by EU rules until the end of 2020, and possibly longer, to allow businesses to adjust
The UK will still pay an estimated £33bn "divorce bill"
The rights of EU citizens living in the UK, and UK citizens in the EU, will be guaranteed

Northern Ireland will be aligned to the EU single market
The controversial "backstop" - that critics feared could have kept the UK in a customs union with the EU indefinitely - has been removed
Northern Ireland will instead remain a part of the UK's customs territory, so it will be included in any future trade deals struck by the government after Brexit
But Northern Ireland will also remain an entry point into the EU's customs zone. The UK will not apply tariffs to products entering Northern Ireland as long as they are not destined for onward transportation across the border
A joint EU/UK committee will decide which goods are at risk of entering the single market and the UK will collect EU tariffs on them on behalf of the EU
The Northern Ireland Assembly - which has been suspended since January 2017 - will get a vote every four years on whether to continue with the new trading arrangements
The decision would be based on a simple majority, rather than requiring a majority of both unionists and nationalists to support the rules in order for them to pass

In a statement, the Democratic Unionists said Northern Ireland's main East-West trade route would still be subject to EU customs rules, "notwithstanding that Northern Ireland will remain part of the UK customs territory".

"All goods would be subject to a customs check regime regardless of their final destination," the statement added, and the plan for a joint EU/UK committee would give the EU a "veto" on which goods would be exempt from tariffs or not.

"This is not acceptable within the internal borders of the United Kingdom," the DUP said.

They expressed concerns Northern Ireland consumers would face increased costs and less choice, and Northern Ireland would also be subject to different VAT arrangements to the rest of the UK.

"Some progress" had been made on democratic consent for the deal, it went on, but the idea of giving the Assembly a vote on the new arrangements that could be won by a "simple majority" violated the Good Friday Agreement, which demands the backing of both unionists and nationalists.

While Boris Johnson may have a deal in Brussels, he absolutely does not have a deal in Westminster.

The DUP isn't prepared to back this package because it does not give it a veto over the new customs arrangement, which it fears could threaten Northern Ireland's position in the United Kingdom.

Team Johnson hopes that, by presenting this as a choice between Mr Johnson's deal and no-deal, the DUP will buckle.

But the DUP doesn't blink easily, and if it doesn't, the signs are Mr Johnson could be defeated on Saturday, when the party's 10 votes could be critical.

That could trigger the Benn Act, forcing a lengthy delay, and could encourage some opposition MP to trigger a motion of no confidence, paving the way for a general election.

It's going to be a titanic tussle on Saturday.

Labour leader Jeremy Corbyn said the deal sounded "even worse" than the one negotiated by the PM's predecessor, Theresa May, and "should be rejected" by MPs.

MPs have voted to hold an extra sitting in the Commons on Saturday to discuss the next steps.

Cabinet Office minister Michael Gove said the government would hold a vote on the deal and was not "not contemplating defeat".

But, he added, if the plan did not get the backing of MPs, the alternative was leaving without a deal.

EU chief negotiator Michel Barnier said he and Mr Juncker had been told by the PM that "he has faith in his ability to convince the majority he needs in the House of Commons".

Brexit Party leader Nigel Farage called for the deal to be rejected by Parliament, saying it would mean "we will not be making our own laws in our own country".

Liberal Democrat leader Jo Swinson said: "The next few days will set the direction of our country for generations, and I am more determined than ever to stop Brexit."

MPs passed a law in September that requires the PM to request an extension on 19 October if Parliament has not agreed a deal or backed leaving without a deal by that date. "

https://www.bbc.co.uk/news/uk-politics-50079385

31st January
91. posted 29 Oct 2019, 00:03

Sigh

Robert Betts
92. posted 29 Oct 2019, 07:54

This is not a particularly new match, I had obviously started looking at him before but stopped as no documentary evidence to back up him having daughters called Sarah and Susan.

Predicted relationship: 5th–8th Cousin to Nephew
Shared DNA: 7 cM across 1 segments

DNA Match

6th cousin of nephew
Robert James Swann 1898-1932
Grandfather of DNA Match
Frederick Swan 1867-1942
Father of Robert James Swann
John Swan 1837-
Father of Frederick Swan
Mary Bather 1812-1888
Mother of John Swan
Susan Betts 1782-
Mother of Mary Bather
Robert Betts 1758-
Father of Susan Betts
Sarah Betts 1785-
Daughter of Robert Betts
John Barber 1822-
Son of Sarah Betts
Julia Barber 1854-
Daughter of John Barber
Florence Louise Martin 1895-1970
Daughter of Julia Barber

Election
93. posted 3 Nov 2019, 09:45

The unsurprising news that due to the Brexit failures there is now going to be another election happened a couple of days ago. I know my cut off for starting book was 31st but like Brexit, I'm just continuing to rumble on...

So had a DNA match that confirmed Timothy Suter again but this one also can confirm William Suter again.

William Suter and Ann Harby had at least 6 children between 1759 and 1772. Of these, one was Timothy and one was Edward.

Edward Suter married Margaret Bains and they had at least 2 children, one of which was Anne in 1810.

Timothy Suter married Ann Freer and they had at least 9 children including Samuel in 1807.

Anne and Samuel were therefore cousins and they married on the 3rd March 1836 and had at least 6 children, one of which was Harriet who was in the DNA match. Explains why 3 hits with such a distant cousin.   (not matched to daughter or nephew)

to son
5th–8th Cousin
Shared DNA: 11 cM across 1 segments

to me
5th–8th Cousin
Shared DNA: 12 cM across 2 segments

to mum
5th–8th Cousin
Shared DNA: 13 cM across 2 segments

Option 1:-

DNA Match
5th Cousin 1x removed to me
Charles Orr Robertson 1933-2011
Grandfather of DNA Match
Lily Orr 1907-1998
Mother of Charles Orr Robertson
Annie Goodwin 1872-1941
Mother of Lily Orr
Harriett Suter 1849-1932
Mother of Annie Goodwin
Samuel Suter 1807-1890
Father of Harriett Suter
Timothy Suter 1772-1851
Father of Samuel Suter
Eliza Suter 1819-1854
Daughter of Timothy Suter
William Henry Turfitt 1840-1920

Son of Eliza Suter

Option 2:-

Harriett Suter 1849-1932
Mother of Annie Goodwin
Anne Suter 1810-1878
Mother of Harriett Suter
Edward Suter 1765-1840
Father of Ann Suter
William Suter 1736-1819
Father of Edward Suter
Timothy Suter 1772-1851
Son of William Suter
Eliza Suter 1819-1854
Daughter of Timothy Suter
William Henry Turfitt 1840-1920
Son of Eliza Suter

George Hoad
94. posted 10 Nov 2019, 11:32

Have a potential match to John Hoad. It really shouldn't matter that I can't confirm connection as I already have matches to him. However I think it might actually to his father, William Hoad.

We know that a George Hoad married Jane Pennels on the 4th December 1848 at Bodiam. This marriage doc gives his father as James Phipps. This indicates he was a bastard. A possible baptism is on the 2nd November 1823 in Dallington. This just gives the mother as Mary Hoad again indicating George was a bastard.

John Hoad and Susannah Manser did have a daughter called Mary in 1766. That would have made her 57 to tie into the baptism doc. I also think she married Thomas Message in 1793 so that would rule her out anyway.

William Hoad and Mary Clapson had several children between 1725 and 1744 including John. Maybe they had another son I don't know about that is the grandfather of George?

Ant & Dec
95. posted 14 Nov 2019, 21:06

There has been a programme on ITV about DNA matches combined with genealogy. It was like WDYTYA but with the added bonus of finding real living distant cousins. The 'experts' do what I do, use the cousin matches to confirm ancestors, especially where the ancestor wasn't known.   The difference between what I do and this programme, is that the cousins are found and then Ant & Dec meet up with them.   Ant had a whole village in Ireland that he was connected to. If the programme was about me they would no doubt fly me to Utah to meet all of the Barber cousins! (170 at last count)

Stupid Northern Monkeys
96. posted 13 Dec 2019, 00:00

So we have had our 2nd referendum and it's a resounding leave. Brexit can proceed. It is really very exciting seeing the swing from Labour to Conservatives in traditional Labour strongholds. Jeremy Corybn has potentially lost more seats than Michael Foot did.

Electoral Reform
97. posted 13 Dec 2019, 07:40

It is not fair that Lib Dems get 11% of the vote and get 11 seats and SNP have 3.9% of vote and get 48 seats. First past the post is not representative.

If the Northerners hadn't voted for the Brexit Party and voted Conservative the Tories would have won even more seats than they did.

Anyway from
https://www.bbc.co.uk/news/election/2019/results:-

PICTURE

Ludovic Colquhoun
98. posted 16 Dec 2019, 21:03

Mary Hutchison was born on the 28th August 1828 in Alloa. She married John Crawford Colquhoun and they had at least 8 children between 1851 and 1868. Mary and John lived in Bonhill all of their lives until 1901 when Mary is in Stirling workhouse.

Their youngest child, Lewis, lived with them until at least 1881. In 1891 he is boarding in Stevenston, Ayrshire and he is working as an analytical chemist. This role took him to Australia and South Africa. At this point Lewis is referred to as Ludovic on all documents. (Cannot find birth doc for Lewis or Ludovic.) According to a shared photo, he married Rosaline Rorich in Durban on the 30th July 1924. Lewis/Ludovic died in 1939 in Pretoria.

DNA Match
4th cousin 1x removed to me
Ludovic Colquhoun 1868-1939
Grandfather of DNA Match
Mary Hutchison 1828-
Mother of Ludovic Colquhoun
Mary Mustart 1797-
Mother of Mary Hutchison
Alexander Mustart 1747-
Father of Mary Mustart
Jean Mustart 1792-1869
Daughter of Alexander Mustart
Alexander Paterson 1825-1865
Son of Jean Mustart

To Daughter
Predicted relationship: 5th–8th Cousin
Shared DNA: 15 cM across 1 segments

To Nephew
Predicted relationship: 5th–8th Cousin

Shared DNA: 15 cM across 1 segments

To Me
Predicted relationship: 5th–8th Cousin
Shared DNA: 17 cM across 1 segments

No match to son

Rejoyce
99. posted 26 Dec 2019, 12:08

Mum had a DNA match that meant I looked into Ann, wife of John Banks again. I knew John Banks married an Ann Banks in Seaford in 1773. I assumed if this was correct that Ann would be his cousin from another Seaford Banks family but never got anywhere with that theory. I now believe that Ann Banks is from an unrelated line coming from Rottingdean then interchanging between Laughton/Ripe/Chiddingley/Rodmell. So based on this match I now have the following extensions:-

Predicted relationship: 5th–8th Cousin
Shared DNA: 6 cM across 2 segments to Mum

DNA Match
6th cousin 1x removed to me
Arthur Lawrence Banks 1886-1945
Grandfather DNA Match
John Thomas Banks 1841-
Father of Arthur Lawrence Banks
Henry Banks 1813-
Father of John Thomas Banks
James Banks 1782-
Father of Henry Banks
William Banks 1739-
Father of James Banks
William Banks 1716-
Father of William Banks
Ann Banks 1743-1841
Daughter of William Banks

Elizabeth Banks 1787-1866
Daughter of Ann Banks
George Green 1817-1886
Son of Elizabeth Banks

Roger Banks 1590-
10th great-grandfather
Thomas Banks 1612-
Son of Roger Banks
Thomas Banks 1646-
Son of Thomas Banks
John Banks 1680-
Son of Thomas Banks
William Banks 1719-
Son of John Banks
Ann Banks 1743-1841
Daughter of William Banks
Elizabeth Banks 1787-1866
Daughter of Ann Banks

Nicholas Butler 1540-
11th great-grandfather
John Butler 1569-
Son of Nicholas Butler
Rejoyce Butler 1607-
Daughter of John Butler
Thomas Banks 1646-
Son of Rejoyce Butler (The name Rejoyce only came up once so pretty sure her surname is Butler)

William Ince 1610-
9th great-grandfather
Elizabeth Ince 1632-
Daughter of William Ince
John Banks 1680-
Son of Elizabeth Ince
William Banks 1719-
Son of John Banks

Ann Banks 1743-1841
Daughter of William Banks

John Bollard 1660-
8th great-grandfather
William Bollard 1680-
Son of John Bollard
Mary Bollard 1704-
Daughter of William Bollard
Ann Banks 1743-1841
Daughter of Mary Bollard

I also wonder if the name Joyce has come from people being called Rejoyce.

£49
100. posted 27 Dec 2019, 09:28

Boxing Day sale on DNA kits, lowest price ever. I'm looking forward to when they are a tenner! I have ordered one. Ideally it would be for sons father so I could do his paternal line but he lives too far away so not going to get his spit. Next option would be to do the in-laws but we aren't close enough to ask for spit. So doing nephews Mum and hoping that being a generation back will get some Swan confirmation. Having my Mum do a test was very helpful for getting back further.

I had a full on Ancestry day yesterday, I had been thinking of cancelling membership. The only thing I want to happen is to get a close paternal match to husband but it's been years now and still only have one 2nd cousin and a Knight line on his paternal side.

The other thing I was thinking of doing instead is a memory book. You pay something like £70 and they email you a question each week. You email back an answer. After 52 questions they send you a printed book of your answers. But I have bought another DNA kit so no money for that this month.

Valentine

Thomas Inwood and Elizabeth Godliman married at St Marys in Marylebone on the 11th May 1772 and had at least 4 children between 1772 and 1779.

One was James born in 1774 and he married Amy or Armey. They had at least 7 children between 1802 and 1827, one was Emma in 1813.

Another was John Inwood born in 1776. He married Mary Ann and they had at least 11 children between 1800 and 1819.

John and Mary Ann had a son called John Valentine Inwood in 1802 but I assume he died as they called a later son John in 1806 and a son called Valentine in 1808. Valentine went on to have a son called James Valentine. (I just find the name Valentine unusual, no other reason for mentioning)

John Inwood Jnr married Emma Inwood, his cousin, c1837. Which was the point of the post.

This lot of Inwood's around Paddington and Marylebone were very poor, They die quite young and usually in workhouses.

Garland
102. posted 30 Dec 2019, 11:29

Been looking at Jane Garling and have decided to delete her parents of William Garling and unknown (subsequent thinking Elizabeth instigated this review).

This means lines Garling and Court and Bowles and Cock have been deleted and replaced with Garland and Partis.

And now a sorry looking:-

PICTURES

The DNA kit arrived a couple of days ago, need to arrange a spit meet. Hope it gets some Brain/Swann line confirmations.

Edward Garland
103. posted 30 Dec 2019, 18:04

So thought I would see if nephew had any matches with Garland in tree. There was about 5 but only 1 that warranted investigation as they were in Tonge, Kent. Turns out Tonge is quite near Lynsted so even if this isn't right, the match must be from this line or it is a big coincidence. Needless to say, this whole Garland line is new:-

Predicted relationship: 5th–8th Cousin to Nephew
Shared DNA: 8 cM across 1 segments

DNA Match
5th cousin 3x removed of nephew
Thomas Tait Garland 1874-1914
Grandfather of DNA Match
William Garland 1843-1915
Father of Thomas Tait Garland (Tate?)
George Garland 1817-1892 (note they have his wife as Mary Ann Hillman, I think it is Mary Ann Pierce)
Father of William Garland
Timothy Garland 1758- (no baptism docs found)
Father of George Garland
Garland - pretty sure Edward
Father of Timothy Garland
William Garland 1755- (several baptism docs found - most likely Edward)
Son of Garland
William Garland 1792-1853
Son of William Garland
Jane Garling 1833-
Daughter of William Garland

Off to see sis-in-law soon for her spit.

Brain Stats

104. posted 31 Dec 2019, 20:57

So far:-

5th Gt Grandparents Thrulines:-

4 John Saddleton/Celia Wraight
2 Israel Steer/Frances Loveland (7)
8 George Tucknott/Lydia Button

Tree (plus wives):-

John Tucknott 1826-1908
George Tucknott 1799-1876
George Tucknott 1760-1846
Samuel Smith 1807
Israel Steer 1783-1864
Henry Charles Martin 1816-1889
Robert Betts 1758
John Robert Saddleton 1856-1915
George Saddleton 1811-1899
John Saddleton 1790-1870
Edward Garland 1720

Test registered and now at the scary part, in the post.

Barber Stats
105. posted 31 Dec 2019, 23:05

Mum may be related to 167 DNA matches through Thomas Barber (and the rest - these are just the ones that have a tree going back to Thomas).

These matches are split as follows by his children:-

Hannah Barber
1821-1864
75 DNA Matches

Eleanor Barber (Mums line)
1825-1867
6 DNA Matches

Henry Barber
1827-1878
22 DNA Matches

Benjamin Barber
1828-1899
23 DNA Matches

Charlotte Barber
1831-1867
1 DNA Match

David Barber
1833-1912
40 DNA Matches

Very obvious the two that did not go to Utah. Have added the Charlotte descendant as having a UK line that isn't my Mums was unusual.

Predicted relationship: 5th–8th Cousin to Mum
Shared DNA: 8 cM across 1 segments

DNA match
4th cousin 1x removed to me
Daisy Jeffery 1891-
Grandmother of DNA Match
John Reuben Jeffery 1853-1940
Father of Daisy Jeffery
Charlotte Barber 1831-1867
Mother of John Reuben Jeffery
Thomas Barber 1793-1862
Father of Charlotte Barber

Charlotte Barber was born in Chiddingley c1831. She married John Jeffrey at St Michaels in Lewes on the 1st September 1847 and they went on to have at least 8 children before she died in 1867. John Jeffrey may then have had 3 children with Jane Follington before marrying her in Icklesham on the 8th September 1878. They then had 4 children in wedlock. In 1891, John is in Hailsham Union Workhouse. His family are living outside of the workhouse suggesting he might be in there for health reasons rather than poverty. It is not clear what happened to him after that but he must have died in the 1890s as Jane is living with her Dad in 1901 and is listed as a widow.

Jane and her son Charles went to Canada on the Empress of Britain, arriving at New Brunswick on the 23rd January 1909. She lived with her son in Kootenay before her death on the 22nd February 1930.

More Lists
106. posted 2 Jan 2020, 19:09

Following on from the Brain post, here are the other lists of the verified ancestors. I have listed the man but it could be his wife or more likely it is both.
Shame I don't have a match for Albert Green 1853-1914 as I would have the entire Green line.
Shame no Gardner verification.
So key targets are husband paternal line, Brain, Swan and Gardner.

Paterson

Stanley Thomas King Paterson 1901-1968
Joseph Charles Paterson 1854-1920
Alexander Mustart 1747
John King 1830-1888
Joseph King 1802-1838
James King 1768-1861
Daniel Evans 1810-1853
Isaac Robbins 1828-1889
William Robbins 1788-1843
Trueman Robinson 1817-1891

Richard Robinson 1769-1836
Edward Storm 1678-1733
Joseph Wickham 1780-1847
John Storm 1740-1813

Green

Ronald Green 1924-1958
Mark Green 1875-1935
George Green 1817-1886
Jesse Green 1786-1873
John Green 1763
Stephen Green 1740-1809
John Green 1712-1770
John Banks 1754-1854
John Banks 1729
William Banks 1719
Jesse Carley 1800-1875
James Carley 1770
Richard Carley 1735-1798
Thomas Bourne 1710
Thomas Barber 1793-1862
Thomas Geall 1735
Thomas Hoad 1772-1838
John Hoad 1735-1824
Benjamin Clapson 1671-1750
Edward Manser 1708
James Gasson 1750
William Henry Turfitt 1840-1920
William Scotney 1758
Timothy Suter 1772-1851
William Suter 1736-1819
William Freer 1750-1829
Henry Freer 1719-1765
George Pell 1799-1866
Robert Pell 1756
John Barber 1778-1861
Frederick Alfred John Snelling 1893-1927
John Shelley 1818-1875

William Shelley 1759
Frederick Taylor 1837
Edward Stapleton 1775-1856
William Malthouse 1746
John Carter 1743
Thomas Sayer Nicholls 1803-1853
John Nicholls 1768-1832
Thomas Sayer 1750
Richard Pettifer 1695
Joseph Cross 1760
Thomas Harris 1810
John Wilson 1801-1886
Francis Wilson 1768

Gardner

William Tee 1830-1905
William Tee 1797-1860
Henry Pittard 1805-1876
William Mardal 1791
Thomas Andrews 1805
Joseph Edward Fearn 1857-1915
John Barnsby 1827-1902
John Goss 1740
Charles Ernest Goodman 1862-1921
James Goodman 1800-1854
William Tredgett 1811-1882
William Tredgett 1788-1864

Maddox

William Maddox 1847-1918
John William Maddox 1805-1878
Richard Martin 1796
Jonathan Mildenhall 1764
Charles George Backhouse 1854-1930
Heinrich Backhaus 1800
John Gouldthorp 1834-1921
Joseph Custerson 1770-1831

John Stafford 1800
John Stafford 1775-1842
James Pratt 1815-1893
Richard Pratt 1753
Joseph Voke 1785
William Henry Pelling 1832
Robert Pelling 1787-1861
Job Wadey 1780
Levi Wadey 1757
Levi Wadey 1728
Robert Alfred Aylen 1843-1935
Thomas Aylen 1770
Henry Stone 1841-1905
John Sperinck 1813-1872

(Harry George Knight 1859-1927)

WTF
107. posted 5 Jan 2020, 21:38

I truly don't understand why the Iranian General, Soleimani, was killed the other day. The only explanation I understand is the meme going round:-

   Trump:- Hey Siri, How many miles did I run today?
   Siri:- Ok, Sending missiles to Iran today

Sigh. I worry about smoking, my tendency to live off crisps and avoid green veg, but hey! WW3 is coming so smoke n snack on!

And whilst America and the Middle East blow each other up, Australia is burning to the ground. There will be no planet left.

Back to my world, a close DNA match with no tree that I messaged about a year ago finally replied! I had given up on ever hearing from them. However not much info to go on so I have asked for clarification. I hope they don't take a year to reply again.

Mary Hopper

108. posted 7 Jan 2020, 22:26

Mary Hopper was baptised at St Marys in Ewell on the 23rd September 1770. Her parents were John and Sarah.

She married Henry Ayling on the 8th May 1795 at St Anne's in Soho. They had a daughter called Esther in 1811. Esther married William Henry Burchett on the 4th May 1835 at St John the Evangelist in Lambeth. They had at least four children including a son, also called William Henry. Esther and William are living with 3 children in 1841 but William Henry Jnr is living with his grandmother, Mary Ayling (Hopper). In 1851, Esther is in Lewisham Workhouse and William Jnr is still living with his grandmother.

Mary Ayling (Hopper), died in Lewisham and was buried at St Marys on the 6th April 1856.

There is no evidence that she married Thomas Aylen or is the mother of Robert Aylen despite what Thrulines/Potential Ancestors say based on 19 public trees.

PICTURE
I think I am actually going to evaluate one of these Thruline hints and press Incorrect.

Robert Aylen
109. posted 8 Jan 2020, 19:52

We know the parents of Robert Alfred Aylen are Robert Aylen and Lucy Saunders as they are on the 1851 census.

We know the father of Robert Aylen (Ayling) is Thomas Aylen (Ayling) as this is on the wedding doc to Lucy Saunders.

There are no documents to find out who the parents of Thomas Aylen (Ayling) are.

There are no Thruline hints for DNA matches for Thomas Aylen. However there are the 10 matches indicated by Mary Hopper. These suggest that Robert may have siblings called John Aylen and Charles Aylen. There isn't any trace of parents for John Aylen. The parents of Charles Aylen are Edward Aylen and Elizabeth Stock. Charles was born on the 28th November 1815 and baptised in Stock in Essex on the 28th January 1816.

As there are DNA matches, it suggests that the parents of John Aylen and Thomas Aylen are also Edward Aylen and Elizabeth Stock but there are no documents to confirm this.

Mary Flux
110. posted 9 Jan 2020, 08:34

Hoping the Xmas presents around the world will result in some more matches. First one of the year, Jane and descendants all new:-

Predicted relationship: 5th–8th Cousin to husband
Shared DNA: 6 cM across 1 segments

DNA Match
6th cousin to husband
Bertha Myrtle Hannam 1910-
Grandmother of DNA Match
William G Hannam 1886-
Father of Bertha Myrtle Hannam
Eliza Smith 1860-
Mother of William G Hannam
Henry Smith 1831-
Father of Eliza Smith
Jane Lewis 1807-
Mother of Henry Smith
Henry Lewis
Father of Jane Lewis
Ann Lewis 1807-1890
Daughter of Henry Lewis
Ann Pitt 1842-1925
Daughter of Ann Lewis
George Aylen 1869-1935
Son of Ann Pitt

Annie Louisa Aylen 1891-
Daughter of George Aylen

The DNA kit I sent has been received and is at processing stage.

Jane Wilkinson
111. posted 9 Jan 2020, 20:00

I have resumed looking at Jane Wilkinson. I was surprised that I did not appear to have done a post about her. I assume there was something in *'Mum....'* and I know when I last looked at her around March 2018, I asked the contact if I could post what she sent me and she never replied. Then of course I go on to the next thing and forget about it.

As I did not get permission to post the contacts findings, I am going to write mine up, which I guess will be pretty similar. Is Jane Wilkinson really Jane Wilkins and therefore the step daughter of Isaac Robbins?

A Jane Robbins is first found in Durham with Isaac Robbins in 1861. She is listed as his daughter, aged 15, born c1846 in Hereson, Pembrokeshire.

On the 20th August 1864, Isaac Robbins, a widowed coal miner aged 34, married a Jane Wilkinson aged 26. This would make her born in 1838. Isaac signs his name but Jane just leaves her mark. They went on to have at least 8 children but it is possible they had at least 2 children before they married.

In 1871, Isaac and Jane are living in Ormesby. Her birth place is Harford West, Pembrokeshire and she is aged 31 making her born in 1840.

In 1881 her birth place is given as Houghton, Pembrokeshire and her age is 36 making her born in 1845. Isaac dies in 1889.

In 1891, Jane is working as a herb beer maker. Her birth location is vague, just Pembrokeshire and she is aged 46 so born in 1845.

In 1901 her birth is given as Parish of Burton, Pembrokeshire, and she is 57 so birth would be c1844.

In 1911 her birth is in Houghton, Pembrokeshire and she is 68 so birth c1843.

On the 16th February 1918, after suffering with pneumonia for 4 days, Jane died. Her occupation on her death certificate was herb beer maker. Her age on her death certificate is 75 so birth c1843. Jane was buried on the 21st February 1918. The gravestone appears to put her age as 79, making her born in 1839:-

"In Loving Memory of ISAAC The beloved husband of JANE ROBBINS Who died March 28th 1889 Aged 60 years Also of THOMAS son of the above Who died January 30th 1888 Aged 28 years Gone but not forgotten Also of JANE The beloved wife if ISAAC ROBBINS Who died February 16th 1918 Aged 79 Years Also of ARTHUR son of the above" rest illegible

It has frustrated me since I started ancestry that I have not been able to find out where and when Jane Wilkinson was born, indeed anything about her before she married Isaac.

There are 4 birth locations, Hereson, Harford West, Houghton and Burton and the date range is 1838-1846. Family search returns the same 3 results for all of them apart from Harford West which returns nothing at all. All 3 results are Wilkins. Absolutely nothing comes up for Wilkinson.

The 3 options are Jane Wilkins 1850, Narberth Pembrokeshire, Jane Wilkin 1846, Pembroke Pembrokeshire and Jane Wilkins 1845, Pembroke Pembrokeshire.

If it was Burton in 1845, then that Jane Wilkins was baptised on the 12th October 1845 and her parents were George Wilkins and Ann Llewellyn. George died in 1849. In 1851, when Jane is 6, she is living with her mother Ann. Then you have the issue that an Ann Wilkins nee Llewellyn married Isaac Robbins on the 23rd November 1854. I cannot locate a death doc for Ann but she presumably died before 1861. This is when I assume that Jane was living with her step father in 1861, hence being called daughter. Jane Wilkins/Wilkinson marries her step father.

Charles Aylen
112. posted 9 Jan 2020, 22:29

Not 100% sure on how this person is connected to my husbands Aylen line. He had 4 wives so even if it turns out he is non blood and the DNA Match is connected some other way, he is still interesting.

Charles Aylen was baptised on the 28th November 1815 in Stock in Essex. His parents were John and Elizabeth. On the 12th July 1835, Charles married Susanna Burchill in Northfleet, Kent. In 1841 they are living in Stifford, Essex. They went on to have at least 5 children before she died in February 1847. Charles married again later that year on the 3rd November to Sarah Malton at St Thomas in Stepney. (Sarah had been previously married to John William Blake.) Charles and Sarah lived in Orsett with his children from his first marriage before she died in 1855.

Charles married again on the 29th August 1856 at Stepney, his third wife was called Rebecca Downs. Rebecca died the following year.

Not one to stay a widower for long, Charles married Susannah Gentry on the 10th November 1857 at St Georges in Bloomsbury.

Charles and Susannah had at least 4 children before she died in 1877. Charles is a farmer and innkeeper all his life. He ran The George in Orsett where he also operated as the village postmaster. On the 6th March 1880, a cottage he owned in South Ockenden was completely destroyed by fire. The fire was believed to be caused by a spark from a passing traction engine. It was ok as his possessions were rescued and he was insured by the Sun Fire Office.

Charles became a prominent member of his local Odd Fellows Society. Charles died on the 13th August 1882 and was buried at St

Giles & All Saints in Orsett, on the 17th. He left £2,061 17s 4d in his will. His son Joseph took over the running of The George.

Neil Peart
113. posted 13 Jan 2020, 23:01

Friday, January 10th, 2020
Neil Peart

It is with broken hearts and the deepest sadness that we must share the terrible news that on Tuesday our friend, soul brother and band mate of over 45 years, Neil, has lost his incredibly brave three and a half year battle with brain cancer (Glioblastoma). We ask that friends, fans, and media alike understandably respect the family's need for privacy and peace at this extremely painful and difficult time. Those wishing to express their condolences can choose a cancer research group or charity of their choice and make a donation in Neil Peart's name. Rest in peace brother.   Neil Peart   September 12, 1952 – January 7, 2020

https://www.rush.com/neil-peart-2/?fbclid=IwAR3KPn_5l2Vr3IlT4V035Jj1PvzLjhkYFkhl8o0cn9LsaA3ovrkYSFHQ-YM

Pheasants
114. posted 19 Jan 2020, 20:57

It being a lovely sunny day, I decided to go to Brightling to see if I could find any Hoad. Carley or Barber gravestones. On the way I drove through Robertsbridge and it looked pretty so I thought I would go back there for lunch. Brightling is not much more than the church and village hall (why do all of these tiny villages have their own hall?) and the St Thomas a Becket church was very easy to find. Having parked near the back I looked at those gravestones first before getting to the actual church. When I went down one side, I was surprised to see a pyramid in the graveyard! This apparently is the grave of John 'Mad Jack' Fuller who I have of course subsequently googled. He was pro slavery so glad to say I doubt he has any connection to me. My ancestors would definitely have known him. There was a pub nearby named after him too.

Most of the gravestones were illegible but there was a Sydney Hoad who appeared to have died in 1982, I haven't got him in my tree so don't know what the connection is. Another was a Herbert James Barber and his wife Violet who both died in the 70s, again they are not in my tree. There is a Robert Stephen Carley and I do have him in my tree! However the stone also has Emily Grace Carley on it and I don't know who she is. He married Margaret Boulton so it is not his wife. The dates would indicate she is his granddaughter? There was also an Alice Bertha Carley but the dates don't match the one in my tree.

I then drove down the road to Etchingham. This was quite residential as this area goes. This church was The Assumption of Blessed Mary & St Nicholas. There were no names of interest in that graveyard.

I then drove back through Brightling to get to Robertsbridge. I had some lunch and went and looked at the very old street. One building was marked 1428 and another had a plaque saying 'The Bough House c1380'.

This is when I rolled my eyes at my knowledge of this area as my next destination was Laughton which was via Brightling. All Saints Church was of no genealogical interest either but it had an interesting stone about Richard Woodman, burnt in Lewes on the 22nd June 1557.

Whilst I drove between Robertsbridge and Brightling all day I saw at least 6 pheasants. Some made me slow down whilst they crossed the road and two made me stop and wait for them to cross.

Although the day didn't turn up much for my tree, it was interesting in other ways.

Inwood
115. posted 23 Jan 2020, 19:44

Results are in. 272 4th cousins or closer and 40 common ancestors.
Most are Tucknott and Saddleton so I haven't looked at them. Sadly
no Brain or Swan. There are a couple of new ones though and this
is the first. Everything from Amy Inwood is new:-

Predicted relationship: 4th–6th Cousin (to sil)
Shared DNA: 25 cM across 1 segments

DNA Match
4th cousin 1x removed (to sil)
Elizabeth Tarrant 1886-
Grandmother of DNA Match
Amy Inwood 1850-1924
Mother of Elizabeth Tarrant
John Inwood 1806-1876
Father of Amy Inwood
John Inwood 1776-
Father of John Inwood
Elizabeth Inwood 1817-
Daughter of John Inwood
Alfred Frederick John Martin 1853-1932
Son of Elizabeth Inwood
Florence Louise Martin 1895-1970
Daughter of Alfred Frederick John Martin
Albert Alfred Tucknott 1924-1973
Son of Florence Louise Martin

Steere
116. posted 23 Jan 2020, 21:41

Had another Inwood, also descendant from Amy. Another new
confirmation, George Steere and his descendants are new:-

Predicted relationship: 5th–8th Cousin (to sil)
Shared DNA: 14 cM across 2 segments

DNA Match
6th cousin (of sil)
Clifford Ridley 1900-1967

Grandfather of DNA Match
Alfred George Ridley 1864-1928
Father of Clifford Ridley
William Ridley 1826-1882
Father of Alfred George Ridley
Elizabeth Steere 1792-1836
Mother of William Ridley
George Steere 1765-
Father of Elizabeth Steere
Edward Steere 1733-
Father of George Steere
Israel Steer 1783-1864
Son of Edward Steere
Mary Ann Steer 1810-1876
Daughter of Israel Steer
Eliza Smith 1831-1901
Daughter of Mary Ann Steer
John Tucknott 1864-1949
Son of Eliza Smith

This also corrected the birth year of Edward Steer. I had something like 1760 because Israel was born in 1783.

Knowlson
117. posted 24 Jan 2020, 19:32

Had another Amy Inwood descendant, taking hers to 3. One of them contacted me today for match clarification. I then had a look at a couple of Wraight hints but they really made no sense, there are too many James Wraights so I gave up on those. So the last new hint. This took far too long to agree due to making mistakes copying the hint. Glad to have got there in the end as this is the nearest to a Brain match that I have:-

Predicted relationship: 5th–8th Cousin (to sil)
Shared DNA: 6 cM across 1 segments

DNA Match
5th cousin 1x removed (of sil)

Robert Henry Caines 1904-1986
Grandfather of DNA Match
William Thomas Caines 1859-
Father of Robert Henry Caines
John Caines 1818-1898
Father of William Thomas Caines
Sarah Knowlson 1794-1874
Mother of John Caines
Thomas Knowlson 1751-1815
Father of Sarah Knowlson
Thomas Knowlson 1792-1849
Son of Thomas Knowlson
Ann Knowlson 1821-1904
Daughter of Thomas Knowlson
Alfred Brain 1848-1908
Son of Ann Knowlson
Joseph Brain 1891-1924
Son of Alfred Brain

Garland
118. posted 24 Jan 2020, 20:55

Now that I have reviewed the common ancestors, I am doing proper
investigations. This is another Knowlson confirmation, everyone
from John Knowlson is new:-

Predicted relationship: 5th–8th Cousin (sil)
Shared DNA: 6 cM across 1 segments

DNA Match
6th cousin (to sil)
Francis Henry Nicholls 1892-1971
Grandfather of DNA Match
Rose Garland 1870-
Mother of Francis Henry Nicholls
Elizabeth Knowlson 1847-
Mother of Rose Garland
John Knowlson 1819-
Father of Elizabeth Knowlson

Charles Knowlson 1778-1846
Father of John Knowlson
Thomas Knowlson 1751-1815
Father of Charles Knowlson
Thomas Knowlson 1792-1849
Son of Thomas Knowlson
Ann Knowlson 1821-1904
Daughter of Thomas Knowlson
Alfred Brain 1848-1908
Son of Ann Knowlson

Yearsley
119. posted 25 Jan 2020, 14:17

Do need to look into Thomas Yearsley a bit more as not sure about
him being married twice (think it is 2 Thomas Yearsleys) but this was
very interesting because it involved Mexico, another Mormon line,
and Joseph Charles Bentley would appear to be a polygamist. I will
write him up next.

Predicted relationship: 5th–8th Cousin (to sil)
Shared DNA: 6 cM across 1 segments

DNA Match
6th cousin 2x removed of sil
Joseph Charles Bentley 1859-1942
Grandfather of DNA Match
Elizabeth Price 1821-1882
Mother of Joseph Charles Bentley
William Price 1791-
Father of Elizabeth Price
Samuel Price 1758-1827
Father of William Price
Mary Yearsley 1726-
Mother of Samuel Price
Thomas Yearsley 1699-
Father of Mary Yearsley
James Yearsley 1745-
Son of Thomas Yearsley

William Yearsley 1775-1841
Son of James Yearsley
Elizabeth Yearsley 1786-1851
Daughter of William Yearsley
Ann Knowlson 1821-1904
Daughter of Elizabeth Yearsley

Chihuahua
120. posted 25 Jan 2020, 14:40

Joseph Charles Bentley was born in Salt Lake City on the 31st August 1859. His parents were Richard (Ricardo) Bentley and Elizabeth Price. Although a document of marriage is not located (the 1900 census says 1880), Joseph married Magdalena (known as Lena) Mickleson. They had at least 8 children between 1881 and 1902. This family appears in the 1900 and 1910 census.

Whilst married to Lena, Joseph married Margaret McLean Ivins on the 30th June 1886. This is the wife he appears to travel to Mexico with. They had at least 3 children between 1899 and 1908, these 3 were all born in Colonia Juarez, Chihuaha, Mexico.

There isn't a wedding doc for Josephs next marriage, public trees have this as 1894. Despite the two other wives that are living, he now marries Gladys Elizabeth Hill Woodmansee. They have at least 2 children, Isaura in 1895 and Harold in 1899.

In 1901, according to public trees, Joseph marries for a fourth time, this time to Maud Mary Taylor. He has at least 3 children with Maud, they were born between 1903 and 1933.

In the 1900 census, Joseph is listed as a preacher but in 1910 he is a general farmer.

He travels to and from Mexico regularly, on the 29th April 1914, 6th December 1917, 25th May 1919, 21st October 1925, 10th February 1931 and 29th March 1941 are all dates when he arrived back in the US.

Of his wives, Gladys died first in 1906, Margaret died in 1928 and
Lena in 1937.

Joseph died on the 7th March 1942 in Colonia Juarez, Chihuaha and
was buried there a day later.

Maud died in 1976.

Juarez Stake of Zion
121. posted 25 Jan 2020, 14:44

From LDS Biographical Encyclopedia:-

"Bentley, Joseph Charles, president of the Juarez Stake of Zion,
Mexico, from 1916 to 1929, was born Aug. 31, 1859, in Salt Lake
City, Utah, a son of Richard Bentley and Elizabeth Price. He was
baptized in 1867, ordained an Elder Jan. 25, 1877, filled a mission to
England in 1879-1881, was ordained a High Priest in 1882, and went
to Mexico in 1892. He acted as Bishop of the Juarez Ward from 1898
to 1916 and was set apart as president of the Juarez Stake May 14,
1916, by Anthony W. Ivins."

Richard Bentley
122. posted 25 Jan 2020, 17:00

The biography of Richard Bentley that is in the book 'Our Pioneer
Heritage - That They May Be Remembered' is 18 pages long. His life
story is very interesting. I don't think I can transcribe 18 pages
though. However I have transcribed one of the two press clippings.
No idea what newspapers they are from.

"RICHARD BENTLEY DEAD

Highly Respected Citizen of St. George Gone to Rest

*Richard Bentley, a highly respected and aged citizen of St. George, died at
his home in that town at an early hour this morning of general debility and old
age. The deceased was born in England in 1820 and was nearly 86 years of age.*

For years he has been very active in the business and church affairs of St. George and had served that community in public office our several occasions, having been mayor several terms and also having occupied other public offices.

He was the pioneer merchant of St. George, having engaged in business there in the early sixties, from which time up to a few years ago he was closely interested in various business enterprises of Washington county. He arrived at Naidoo from England in 1843 and came to Salt Lake in the early fifties and resided in the Seventeenth ward for many years. During his residence in this city he was employed in the Historian's office.

From Salt Lake he went to Carson City, Nev., which at that time was included within the boundaries of this territory where, with a colony of Saints he settled that community. Upon his return to Utah he located at Nephi and was in that town during the Indian troubles. From Nephi he moved to St. George where he purchased the home of Apostle Pratt, in which he resided at the time of his death.

The deceased leaves a widow, six children, 40 grandchildren and 10 great grandchildren. His three sons are William Oscar and Frank R who reside at St. George, and Joseph C.Bentley, who resides in Mexico. His daughters are Mrs. E.G. Woolley of this city, Mrs. E.D. Wooley of Kanab, and Mrs. Nesion Terry of Enterprise. The arrangements for the funeral have not yet been announced."

Hannah Brain
123. posted 26 Jan 2020, 09:34

I got excited when I saw a match that mainly came from Bitton. However, I have no idea how Hannah is connected to my William Brain as the match appears to have gone wrong after Hannah:-

Predicted relationship: 5th–8th Cousin to sil
Shared DNA: 14 cM across 1 segments

DNA Match - CONNECTION NOT ESTABLISHED YET
8th cousin to sil
Ivy Irene Davis 1910-1966
Grandmother of DNA Match

Emma Carter 1874-1943
Mother of Ivy Irene Davis
Henry Willis Carter 1839-1900
Father of Emma Carter
Kezia Willis 1815-1895
Mother of Henry Willis Carter
Hannah Brain 1780-1861
Mother of Kezia Willis
***Joseph Brain 1760-**
Father of Hannah Brain*
Moses Brain 1726-
Father of Joseph Brain
William Brain 1700-
Father of Moses Brain
William Brain 1729-
Son of William Brain
William Brain 1762-
Son of William Brain
William Brain 1782-1848
Son of William Brain
James Rider Brain 1813-1847
Son of William Brain
Alfred Brain 1848-1908
Son of James Rider Brain

(All new from William Brain 1729)

Hannah Brain was born c1780 in Hanham according to the 1841, 1851 and 1861 census.

On the 26th April 1805, Hannah married Thomas Willis in Bitton. Hannah and Thomas went on to have at least 4 children. Hannah died in Gloucs. on the 30th November 1861 and she left under £20 to her son Johnathon.

There are no documents confirming her parents as there are 6 options of a Hannah Brain being born in Bitton c1780 and none give the father as Joseph.

Exact year matches are:-

30 Jan 1780 Ruardean William & Ann
1 Nov 1780 Newnham Robert & Elizabeth
1 Oct 1780 Dodington Job & Mary

Nearer locations are:-

29 Dec 1777 Bitton Thomas & Sarah
26 Nov 1781 Bitton Robert & Ann
16 Jan 1785 Bitton Samuel & Amey

My favourite would be 1781 Bitton, unlikely to be the other 2 Bitton but it could be any of the other matches.

I think it is too much of a coincidence to think the match is connected any other way. It will be a challenge to find the link.

John Tasker
124. posted 30 Jan 2020, 07:54

A match that had shared matches indicating a Robbins/Wilkins/Llewellyn connection contacted me. I didn't think I would establish a connection because I did not recognise any names in the tree and one line, Tasker, stops abruptly as it is known that John Tasker was illegitimate. Still can't resist a challenge, especially when I saw John came from Burton. Haven't found the connection yet but in just an hour, I found out he is really John Wilkins, there must be some connection to my Jane Wilkins(on)!

A William Wilkins was baptised in Burton on the 30th July 1851. His mother was Ann Wilkins with no father given. No idea what happened to William because the name is so common.

A John Wilkins was baptised in Burton on the 21st March 1855. His mother was Ann Wilkins with no father given. In 1861, aged just 6, he is listed as a 'boarder' at the Tasker house in St Marys, Pembrokeshire. How is John connected to the Taskers? Or are they just sort of fostering/adopting a random child? There is an Ann there but I believe George Tasker married an Ann Griffiths or Ann Hopkins, not an Ann Wilkins. Also the children of George and Ann are older than John.

By 1871, John Wilkins is calling himself John Tasker. However he is not living with the Tasker family anymore, he is in lodgings. John is a labourer for a boiler maker.

I cannot find a marriage doc for John with Wilkins or Tasker, however he married a Louisa c 1876 and they went on to have at least 8 children. In 1881 he is a labourer and in 1891 he is a 'Dock Constable' which he also is in 1901. I cannot find him in 1911. John may have died in Swansea in 1930.

Wilkins
125. posted 30 Jan 2020, 21:03

Given the level of DNA matches to back up the theory, I have added Ann and her descendants to my tree. No documentation link Ann & George.

Daughter - surprisingly high:-
Predicted relationship: 5th–8th Cousin
Shared DNA: 17 cM across 2 segments

Son - as usual on Paterson line, quite low:-
Predicted relationship: 5th–8th Cousin
Shared DNA: 7 cM across 1 segments

Nephew:-
Predicted relationship: 5th–8th Cousin
Shared DNA: 10 cM across 2 segments

Me - really high:-
Predicted relationship: 4th–6th Cousin
Shared DNA: 21 cM across 3 segments

DNA Match to me
4th cousin 1x removed

Annie Tasker 1884-1972
Grandmother of DNA Match
John Wilkins/Tasker 1854-
Father of Annie Tasker
Ann Wilkins c1825-
Mother of John Wilkins
Wilkins c1790-* no docs matching Ann & George
Father of Ann Wilkins
George Wilkins 1820-1849
Son of Wilkins
Jane Wilkinson 1845-1918
Daughter of George Wilkins

31st January 2020
126. posted 31 Jan 2020, 20:51

It's been a nice month or so Brexit wise as it hasn't been very newsworthy. Boris with his majority got his Brexit bill passed quickly and quietly. So today in just over 2 hours we enter the transition period. Eleven months left.

Zipporah
127. posted 3 Feb 2020, 23:23

I cannot find a link between Joshua Lenny and Simon Lenny. Thrulines suggest that Joshua is the son of Simon but given birth dates I would think it more likely they are brothers. If I only had one match I probably would wonder but there are 2 both from Clarissa Lenny. Always strange when parents don't get same matches as their children.

Predicted relationship: 5th–8th Cousin to sil
Shared DNA: 6 cm across 1 segment

DNA Match
5th cousin of sil
Elizabeth Baldry 1877-
Grandmother of DNA Match
Harriet Gardener 1847-

Mother of Elizabeth Baldry
Clarissa/Clara Lenny 1813-1895
Mother of Harriet Gardener
Simon Lenny 1775-1838
Father of Clarissa Lenny
Lenny no connection found
Father of Simon Lenny
Joshua Lenny 1785-1812
Son of Lenny
Maria Lenny 1813-
Daughter of Joshua Lenny
Julia Barber** 1854-
Daughter of Maria Lenny
Florence Louise Martin 1895-1970
Daughter of Julia Barber

Predicted relationship: 5th–8th Cousin to nephew
Shared DNA: 11 cm across 1 segment

DNA Match
6th cousin of nephew
Daniel William Gardner 1911-2003
Grandfather of DNA Match
William Gardner 1877-1955
Father of Daniel William Gardner
Daniel Gardener 1842-1913
Father of William Gardner
Clarissa/Clara Lenny 1813-1895
Mother of Daniel Gardener
Simon Lenny 1775-1838
Father of Clarissa Lenny
Lenny no connection found
Father of Simon Lenny
Joshua Lenny 1785-1812
Son of Lenny
Maria Lenny 1813-
Daughter of Joshua Lenny
Julia Barber** 1854-
Daughter of Maria Lenny

Florence Louise Martin 1895-1970
Daughter of Julia Barber

** Public trees suggest Sarah Hurring/Hurren is descendant from a local Barber line too so there maybe a more distant connection as well

Simon Lenny married Sarah Hurring in Bramfield, Suffolk on the 26th March 1798. They went on to have at least 10 children and gave them some amazing names:-

    Phoebe Lenny 1798–
    Bathsheba Lenny 1801–
    Elizabeth Lenny 1802–
    Louisa Lenny 1806–
    Simon Lenny 1808–
    Clarissa/Clara Lenny 1813–1895
    Septima Lenny 1814–
    Esau Lenny 1816–
    Zipporah Lenny 1818–
    Octavia Lenny 1819–

Simon died in Blything in 1838. Sarah died in 1852.

Hailstone
128. posted 5 Feb 2020, 07:02

Phoebe Lenny was born on the 21st June 1798 in Suffolk and baptised in Bramfield on the 16th December. Phoebe married Hailstone Pretty (Pritty) on the 28th May 1822 and they went on to have at least 7 children before Phoebe died in 1841, presumably giving birth.

No point to this post apart from what a cool name is Hailstone?!?

Hailstone married again to Charlotte Gooch and they had at least 6 children before he died in 1883.

William Clark

129. posted 5 Feb 2020, 19:30

Son has a new line match and quite a close one. This line has been sort of verified at a later stage via the Mardells but this is the first Clark confirmation.

William Clark is the son of Daniel Clark and Rose Mardell and was baptised in Welwyn on the 21st November 1858. William married Harriet Haggar on the 3rd October 1880. Harriet died in 1896. William then married Elizabeth Andrews c1897 and they went on to have at least 3 children. William worked as a bootmaker specifically a 'shoe laster'. William died in St Albans in 1930. Most of this was probably already in *'Mum....'* but the death date is new, the match had a copy of his death certificate.

Predicted relationship: 4th–6th Cousin to son
Shared DNA: 68 cm across 4 segments

DNA Match
2nd cousin 1x removed of son
Violet Clark 1897-1980
Grandmother of DNA Match
William Clark 1858-1930
Father of Violet Clark
Daisy Clark 1898-1958
Daughter of William Clark
Robert William Gardner 1926-2000
Son of Daisy Clark

Angels
130. posted 11 Feb 2020, 19:30

Two Thrulines confirming an Aylen that wasn't confirmed before for husband:-

Predicted relationship: 5th–8th Cousin
Shared DNA: 8cm across 1 segment

DNA Match

4th cousin 1x removed
Annie Angell 1903-
Grandmother of DNA Match
Annie Aylen 1874-
Mother of Annie Angell
Thomas Aylen 1845-
Father of Annie Aylen
Robert Aylen 1815-
Father of Thomas Aylen
Robert Alfred Aylen 1843-1935
Son of Robert Aylen
George Aylen 1869-1935
Son of Robert Alfred Aylen
Annie Louisa Aylen 1891-
Daughter of George Aylen

Predicted relationship: 5th–8th Cousin
Shared DNA: 16cm across 1 segment

DNA Match
3rd cousin 2x removed
Annie Aylen 1874-
Grandmother of DNA Match
Thomas Aylen 1845-
Father of Annie Aylen
Robert Aylen 1815-
Father of Thomas Aylen
Robert Alfred Aylen 1843-1935
Son of Robert Aylen
George Aylen 1869-1935
Son of Robert Alfred Aylen
Annie Louisa Aylen 1891-
Daughter of George Aylen

Josiah Andrews
131. posted 11 Feb 2020, 21:20

I made an error which meant that some DNA matches and Thrulines made no sense to me. I had my sons 3rd Gt Grandfather, Josiah Andrews, as marrying Mary Ann Forster. He actually married Mary Ann Haggar on the 18th April 1874 at St Andrews in Radwinter, Essex. This gives me:-

Matthew Saggers 1700-
8th great-grandfather of son
John Saggers 1734-
Son of Matthew Saggers
Thomas Saggers 1755-
Son of John Saggers
Jane Saggers 1790-1847
Daughter of Thomas Saggers
Samuel Haggar 1817-1887
Son of Jane Saggers
Mary Ann Haggar* 1854-
Daughter of Samuel Haggar
Elizabeth Andrews 1875-
Daughter of Mary Ann Hagger
Daisy Clark 1898-1958
Daughter of Elizabeth Andrews

*I had Forster

Sammy Hagar
132. posted 11 Feb 2020, 22:06

Predicted relationship: 4th–6th Cousin to son
Shared DNA: 35cm across 2 segments

DNA Match
4th cousin 1x removed of son
Arthur Joseph Elsom 1910-2005
Grandfather of DNA Match
Arthur Elsom 1884-1935
Father of Arthur Joseph Elsom
Elizabeth Hagger 1862-
Mother of Arthur Elsom

Samuel Haggar 1817-1887
Father of Elizabeth Hagger
Mary Ann Hagger 1854-
Daughter of Samuel Haggar
Elizabeth Andrews 1875-
Daughter of Mary Ann Hagger
Daisy Clark 1898-1958
Daughter of Elizabeth Andrews

This has been bugging me since he got his results as match tree set to private. Don't think I've ever asked for access though. Samuel and Elsom line all new.

Op
133. posted 13 Feb 2020, 21:59

I had sort of planned to write a history of my periods but not in mood right now. Anyway, after the successful Zoladex trial last year, I am now having my tubes removed. I think it is called a salpingectomy. I am a bit nervous about the op but mostly annoyed that if I could have had this done 10 years ago, the lives of 4 people would have been very different. I'm supposed to look at the positives, going forwards I will be ok. But I am nearly at menopause age so how much reprieve am I being given? Could be one month or five years. All I know is I am never ever going to forgive the bitch GP who patronisingly tapped my knee and said "I get PMT too dear". Fucking cow.

Moorsom
134. posted 22 Feb 2020, 21:18

New RH Bay match! To me, daughter and nephew but not son:-

Predicted relationship: 5th–8th Cousin to d
Shared DNA: 14 cm across 1 segment

Predicted relationship: 5th–8th Cousin to n
Shared DNA: 11cm across 1 segment

Predicted relationship: 5th–8th Cousin to me
Shared DNA: 12cm across 1 segment

DNA Match
5th cousin to me
Gladys Parkinson 1912-1987
Grandmother of DNA Match
Florence Mary Buff 1890-
Mother of Gladys Parkinson
Isabella Moorsom 1851-1930
Mother of Florence Mary Buff
Greenup Moorsom 1819-
Father of Isabella Moorsom
Greenup Moorsom 1779-1837
Father of Greenup Moorsom
Jane Moorsom 1817-1896
Daughter of Greenup Moorsom
George Robinson 1844-1907
Son of Jane Moorsom
Alice Robinson 1870-1940
Daughter of George Robinson

I obviously survived the op. At present I can't say it has worked as
had headache all week and that sent me into a spiral of depression.

Robinson
135. posted 22 Feb 2020, 21:54

It appears that the wife of Greenup Moorsom that I only had as Mary
before is actually Mary Robinson so a match to the Robinson line
too:-

Mary Robinson
wife of 4th Gt Uncle

now also 4th Gt Aunt

DNA Match
5th cousin to me

Gladys Parkinson 1912-1987
Grandmother of DNA Match
Florence Mary Buff 1890-
Mother of Gladys Parkinson
Isabella Moorsom 1851-1930
Mother of Florence Mary Buff
Mary Robinson 1820-1855
Mother of Isabella Moorsom
George Robinson 1794-1824
Father of Mary Robinson
Trueman Robinson 1817-1891
Son of George Robinson
George Robinson 1844-1907
Son of Trueman Robinson
Alice Robinson 1870-1940
Daughter of George Robinson

Not surprised by duplicate match as despite no match to son, the match to us three was quite high for a 5th cousin

10th Cousin
136. posted 23 Feb 2020, 11:52

This is in no way verified. I had Thomas Storm and his son Thomas, who both died whilst fishing in 1686, rest is from match tree:-

Predicted relationship: 5th–8th Cousin
Shared DNA: 7cm across 1 segment

DNA Match
10th cousin
Dorothy Maud Shaw 1910-1979
Grandmother of DNA Match
John Henry Shaw 1872-
Father of Dorothy Maud Shaw
Henry Shaw 1840-
Father of John Henry Shaw
Margaret Brown Storm 1805-1866
Mother of Henry Shaw

Matthew Storm 1784-
Father of Margaret Brown Storm
Matthew Storm 1740-1819
Father of Matthew Storm
Thomas Storm
Father of Matthew Storm
Matthew Storm
Father of Thomas Storm
Thomas Storm 1661-1686
Father of Matthew Storm
Thomas Storm 1635-1686
Father of Thomas Storm
Mary Storm 1671-1750
Daughter of Thomas Storm
William Storm 1699-1774
Son of Mary Storm
John Storm 1740-1813
Son of William Storm
Elizabeth Storm 1771-1846
Daughter of John Storm
John Hodgson Storm 1791-1861
Son of Elizabeth Storm
Betsey (Elizabeth) Storm 1814-1883
Daughter of John Hodgson Storm
Mary Ann Wickham 1843-1916
Daughter of Betsey (Elizabeth) Storm
Alice Robinson 1870-1940
Daughter of Mary Ann Wickham

Isabella Moorsom
137. posted 23 Feb 2020, 13:50

Isabella is one of at least 5 children of Greenup Moorsom and Mary
Robinson. She was born in RHB in 1851 and baptised on the 30th
March 1851. She lived with her family until at least 1871. Her family
had moved from RHB to Durham by 1861. In 1872 she married
James Johnson Armstrong in Hartlepool. James died in 1881, they
do not appear to have had any children. In 1881, Isabella lived with
her in laws in Durham. In 1886 she married Reuben Buff and they

had at least two children before he died in 1891.   In 1897, Isabella married again, this time to George Pallin. George died two years later.

In 1901, Isabella and her two children, Reuben Buff and Florence Mary Buff, were in Hartlepool Union Workhouse.

By 1911 they were out of the workhouse and Isabella worked as a confectioner.

Isabella died in Hartlepool in 1930.

Not 10th Cousin
138. posted 23 Feb 2020, 14:22

A much more realistic 5th:-

Predicted relationship: 5th–8th Cousin
Shared DNA: 7cm across 1 segment

DNA Match
5th cousin
Gladys Parkinson 1912-1987
Grandmother of DNA Match
Florence Mary Buff 1890-1924
Mother of Gladys Parkinson
Isabella Moorsom 1851-1930
Mother of Florence Mary Buff
Mary Robinson 1820-1855
Mother of Isabella Moorsom
George Robinson 1794-1824
Father of Mary Robinson
Trueman Robinson 1817-1891
Son of George Robinson
George Robinson 1844-1907
Son of Trueman Robinson
Alice Robinson 1870-1940
Daughter of George Robinson

I have no evidence of who my 4th Gt Grandfather is apart from what I had obtained from Storm & Co so many many years ago. According to Storm & Co he is Greenup Moorsom, born in RHB in 1779 and died on the 24th May 1837. His wife was Isabella Richardson. Their children's baptisms (where found) confirm their parents names though and Isabella is also found on the census.

Greenup Moorsom (1) and Isabella had a son called Greenup Moorsom (2) in RHB on the 30th August 1808. Greenup (2) was baptised on the 28th October 1808. He died less than a year later on the 17th May 1809.

Greenup (1) and Isabella also named their last son Greenup Moorsom (3). Greenup (3) was born on the 17th October 1819 in RHB. In 1841, Greenup (3) is living with his mother Isabella and his older brother William. His occupation is 'mariner'. In 1842 he marries Mary Robinson. (I am still not 100% sure where she fits in with my Robinson line, if at all, as the only documents found are the wedding doc and the 1841 census where she is living alone, there are no documents giving her parents.) On the 18th January 1851, Greenup (3), was issued with his master mariner certificate. Mary and Greenup (3) had at least 5 children before she died in 1855. Greenup (3), remarried on the 11th August 1859 in London to Elizabeth Brightwell Smith. Greenup (3) and Elizabeth had at least 3 children before he died c1866-1874.

Greenup Moorsom (4) was the son of Greenup (3) and Mary. He was born in RHB in 1844 and baptised on the 3rd March. Greenup (4) married Ann Jefferson at Holy Trinity in Hartlepool on the 10th March 1866. Greenup (4) and Ann had a daughter, Ethel Annie Moorsom.

In 1881, Greenup (4) is the master of the S.S. Wave and he obtains his masters certificate on the 8th January 1890. Greenup (4) died on the 1st October 1910 and he left his daughter Ethel, £289 11s.

Ethel Annie Moorsom married James William Storm in 1899. They went on to have at least 5 children, one of which was Greenup Moorsom Storm (5).

(James William Storm was the son of Jacob Storm (1838-1926) and Isabel Pearson who were already in my tree. Jacob Storm was at that point coming up as "husband of sister-in-law of 3rd great-aunt" but because of this marriage he is now my 'father in law of 2nd cousin 3x removed'.)

Greenup (5) was born on the 25th November 1901. He received a medal for his merchant navy service in WW1. He married Constance Muriel Bramald on the 1st September 1928. Greenup (5) died in 1975.

Another 5th
140. posted 23 Feb 2020, 17:11

Only me and nephew match this one, I know I don't type up double confirmations usually but as I'm looking at this line anyway:-

5th-8th Cousin to me
Shared DNA 15cm across 1 segment

5th-8th Cousin to n
Shared DNA 11cm across 1 segment

DNA Match
5th cousin to me
Harry Storm 1897-1978
Grandfather of DNA Match
Ethel Annie Moorsom 1880-1964
Mother of Harry Storm
Greenup Moorsom 1844-1910
Father of Ethel Annie Moorsom
Mary Robinson 1820-1855
Mother of Greenup Moorsom
George Robinson 1794-1824
Father of Mary Robinson

Trueman Robinson 1817-1891
Son of George Robinson
George Robinson 1844-1907
Son of Trueman Robinson

BBC LGBTQ+
141. posted 24 Feb 2020, 07:25

My morning consists of tea n toast and reading the news. Today this included reading about Douglas Byng:-

"1938

Douglas Byng is the first female impersonator on television. He later has his own shows including Byng Ho! and Queue for a Song.

He never retires, and in 1977 at the age of 90 appears on Parkinson and Radio 4.

Within his own theatrical world, Byng is openly gay but very discreet outside it. He stars in music hall, revue and cabaret."

https://www.bbc.com/historyofthebbc/lgbtq/lgbtq-timeline#thescanwemention

I was recently contacted by a much closer relative to Douglas. If I was weirded out seeing his name, they must find it weirder. I don't think I would like to be in the news or famous for anything.

John Goodman
142. posted 27 Feb 2020, 07:18

Son has another Goodman ancestor verified:-

Predicted relationship: 5th–8th Cousin
Shared DNA: 14 cm across 1 segment

DNA Match

3rd cousin 1x removed of son
Florence Emma Goodman 1893-1967
Grandmother of DNA Match
William Goodman 1865-
Father of Florence Emma Goodman
John Goodman 1834-1884
Father of William Goodman
Charles Ernest Goodman 1862-1921
Son of John Goodman
Jessie Goodman 1898-
Daughter of Charles Ernest Goodman
Doreen Joan Fearn 1929-1985
Daughter of Jessie Goodman

Had to Florence already, her descendants are new.

Lucas
143. posted 27 Feb 2020, 09:13

Sister in Law has potentially verified the Luckhurst line. Nephew does not seem to have this match. This common ancestor hint was based on public trees and it all ties in with documents apart from the illegitimate Florence Ada Harnett*. I am not paying for a birth certificate for a distant cousin to only see that father is blank so going to have to take the public trees as confirmation that Henry John Packer** is her father. Before she marries she is living with her Uncle and Aunt on her mothers side so the census is no help.

Another interesting development I want to pursue is that the baptism doc of Frances Ann Luckhurst*** gives her name as Lucas not Luckhurst.

Predicted relationship: 5th–8th Cousin to sil
Shared DNA: 8cm across 1 segment

DNA Match
6th cousin to sil
Percy Francis Spratt 1898-1978
Grandfather of DNA Match

Florence Ada Harnett* 1871-1965
Mother of Percy Francis Spratt
Henry John Packer** 1848-1930
Father of Florence Ada Harnett
Henry Hillard Packer 1823-1864
Father of Henry John Packer
Frances Ann Luckhurst*** 1788-
Mother of Henry Hillard Packer
Daniel Luckhurst -1841
Father of Frances Ann Luckhurst
Daniel Luckhurst 1787-1855
Son of Daniel Luckhurst
George Luckhurst 1828-1905
Son of Daniel Luckhurst
Elizabeth Esther Luckhurst 1861-1939
Daughter of George Luckhurst
George G Saddleton 1900-
Son of Elizabeth Esther Luckhurst

Strangers
144. posted 27 Feb 2020, 09:30

Well it might not be my sils Daniel Luckhurst but there is a Daniel Lucas born on the 15th July 1752, baptised at Walloon or Strangers Church, Canterbury on the 19th July 1752. His parents were Daniel Lucas and Angelique Largilier. This implies that Angelique at least was a French Huguenot.

http://www.frenchchurchcanterbury.org.uk/history/strangers-in-canterbury.html

Huguenots
145. posted 27 Feb 2020, 10:51

If (IF) Luckhurst is Lucas then his French ancestors were as follows (church in brackets) (maternal in italics):-

Jaques Lucas (Francois Canteau)
9th great-grandfather of nephew

Jaques Lucas (Threadneedle Street French Huguenot) 1687-
(Catherine Battaille)
Son of Jaques Lucas
Daniel Lucas (Walloon Church Canterbury) 1722- (Angelique
L'Argillere)
Son of Jaques Lucas
Daniel Luckhurst/Lucas (Walloon Church Canterbury) 1752-
1841
Son of Daniel Lucas

Can't find anything on the maternal lines.

It is a fair assumption to say that Jaques Lucas and Francois Canteau
emigrated to England in October 1685 with the other 50,000
protestants Louis XIV effectively kicked out.

Dreadnought
145. posted 27 Feb 2020, 13:24

Henry John Packer is the son of Henry Hilliard (Hillard/Hilyard) and
Caroline Frances Bell. He was born in 1848 and lived with his family
in Seasalter and Whitstable until at least 1861.

At some point he joined the Navy and he served on HMS Jason. He
was serving on this ship when he was court martialled on the 27th
November 1867. I cannot see anything else on that matter as it is
part of Fold3 which I have to pay more for.

In 1869, Henry married Fanny Jane Holden in Blean. In 1871 they
were living with Henry's mum and siblings and his occupation is a
mariner.

Then according to public trees he had an illegitimate daughter,
Florence Ada Harnett, with Sarah Harnett later that year.

In 1874, Henry and Fanny have a daughter of their own, Bessie Maud
Packer. Fanny & Bessie do not appear on any census with him but
he is a sailor so not unusual.

In 1881 he is an Able Seaman on the Woldemar. On the 16th April 1881 he was admitted to Dreadnoughts Seaman Hospital with venereal disease. At the time he was serving on the Dagmar from Cardiff to Whitstable. He stayed for 47 days being discharged as cured on the 1st June.

I cannot locate him in 1891. On the 1901 census he is a mate on the Faithlee which was docked in Ramsgate Harbour at the time.

On the 15th March 1906, Henry was admitted to Dreadnoughts hospital again. At this point, he was a mate on the Eleanor sailing to and from Yarmouth. He stayed for 10 days until he was cured of something illegible that looks like it might say erysipelas which is a bacterial infection.

In 1908, his wife Fanny dies. In 1911, he is living at the Blean Union Workhouse. Henry died in Blean in 1930. I think going by the court martial and the VD, and the lack of evidence he was involved with Fanny & Bessie, it is likely that Florence was his daughter. Was Sarah a prostitute?

George Wigzell
146. posted 27 Feb 2020, 20:17

Daniel Luckhurst and Elizabeth Diplock had at least 14 children between 1810 and 1828, 2 of which were Fanny (1816) and Charlotte (1817). They were all born in Sevenoaks.

John Wigzell and Dinah Lee, also from Sevenoaks, had at least 2 children, George (1812) and John (1818).

On the 21st December 1838, John Wigzell (Jnr) married Charlotte Luckhurst at St Marys in Newington, Surrey. In 1844, his brother John married Charlottes sister, Fanny Luckhurst at Whitechapel.

The Luckhursts are the blood connection and I only looked at the Wigzells to check they were brothers initially. I always am intrigued when it looks like sisters from one family marry brothers from

120

another. Turned out the husband George Wigzell is interesting so I am going to write him up. He has his own (rather sparse) wiki page:-

"George Wigzell (6 May 1812 – 1875) was an English first-class cricketer active 1849–60 who played for the Lancashire county cricket teams organised by Manchester Cricket Club; and for Kent County Cricket Club. He was born in Sevenoaks and died in Bonham, Fannin County, Texas. He played in eleven first-class matches, taking 42 wickets."

https://en.wikipedia.org/wiki/George_Wigzell

George Wigzell was born in Sevenoaks on the 6th May 1812 and baptised on the 5th August. He married Charlotte Luckhurst at St Marys on the 21st December 1838. George and Charlotte went on to have at least 6 children before she died in 1850. In 1851 he is working as a brewer and he has a servant called Sarah Scott. On the 5th June 1852 he married Sarah Scott at Hinksey in Oxfordshire. George was playing County Cricket by 1849 and he continued until 1860. His matches were as follows:-

23 JUL 1849 County Match, County Match 1849 Hyde Park Ground, Sheffield. - 1, Yorkshire
Yorkshire CCC, Yorkshire - Won by 5 wickets
02 AUG 1849 County Match, County Match 1849 Botanical Gardens, Manchester. - 1, Lancashire
Yorkshire CCC, Yorkshire - Won by 10 wickets
05 JUL 1852 England Other First-Class matches, Other First-Class matches 1852 Lord's(Lord's Cricket Ground)St John's Wood Road, London. - 1, Middlesex
England, ENG - Won by 7 wickets
16 AUG 1852 England Other First-Class matches, Other First-Class matches 1852 Spitfire Ground(St Lawrence Ground), Canterbury. - 1, Kent
England, ENG - Won by 10 wickets
16 JUN 1859 County Match, County Match 1859 John Walker's Ground, Southgate (The Walker Cricket Ground)(Chapel Fields). - 1, Bedfordshire
Middlesex CCC, Middlesex - Won by 78 runs

23 JUN 1859 England Other First-Class matches, Other First-Class matches 1859 Mote Park, Maidstone. - 1, Kent
Kent CCC, Kent - Won by 10 wickets
25 JUL 1859 County Match, County Match 1859 Spitfire Ground(St Lawrence Ground), Canterbury. - 1, Kent
Middlesex CCC, Middlesex - Won by 10 wickets
28 JUL 1859 County Match, County Match 1859 Higher Common Ground, Tunbridge Wells - 1, Kent
Sussex CCC, Sussex - Won by 6 wickets
01 AUG 1859 County Match, County Match 1859 Royal Brunswick Ground, Hove - 1, Sussex
Sussex CCC, Sussex - Won by 169 runs
08 AUG 1859 England Other First-Class matches, Other First-Class matches 1859 The Kia Oval (Kennington Oval;The Oval; The AMP Oval; The Foster's Oval; The Brit Oval), London. - 1, Surrey
Surrey CCC, Surrey - Won by 10 wickets
14 JUN 1860 England Other First-Class matches, Other First-Class matches 1860 Lord's(Lord's Cricket Ground)St John's Wood Road, London. - 1, Middlesex
Kent CCC, Kent - Won by 7 wickets

https://mobile.crichq.com/players/1708073-george-wigzell/matches

The site above has a lot more stats about these matches and George Wigzell, if you understand and are into that sort of thing. I think the most noticeable win is Kent against England in 1859 at Mote Park, his sides seem to have lost a lot.

George and Sarah had at least 7 children in this time period. In 1861, George appears to have the rather odd job title of 'formerly wine merchant'.

Whether 'formerly' meant unemployed and broke or retired and comfortable, by the mid 1860's he is thinking of going to America. A public tree has this rather interesting excerpt from the Maidstone Journal and Kentish Advertiser dated 24th December 1866:-

"George Wigzell (Kentish Cricketer) formerly of Sevenoaks, having a wife and ten children, has an opportunity of emigrating to the United States in the beginning of January, through the kindness of a gentleman who will pay half the passage money, and find them employment also, if the other half amounting to £50, can be raised.

Donations received by Mr Silas Corke, Auctioneer, Sevenoaks."

George must have raised the money but didn't leave in January so maybe not by then. Did he lose the other half of the money as he didn't raise the rest in time or did the gentleman wait? Either way, George and his family left England on the Tarifa, arriving at New York on the 5th November 1867.

By 1870, he was working as a farmer in Washington Texas. His wife is given as Mary but although the document is really clear I can't see how it isn't Sarah. His wife Sarah, although not found in 1870 is living in Texas with their children in 1880.

The public trees and wiki page say George died in Bonham, Fannin, Texas in 1875.   The public trees say Sarah died in 1906.

Sarah Low
147. posted 5 Mar 2020, 07:13

This common ancestor hint did not have the matches tree as back up and I am currently quite confused as to who Richard Roots married and when Sarah Low (his first or only wife) died. What is definite is that their son John Low Roots gave the middle name Low to his 6 children:-

5th–8th Cousin to son
Shared DNA: 7 cM across 1 segments

DNA Match
6th cousin of son
Dorothy Louise Roots 1902-1985
Great Grandmother of DNA Match
Henry Low Roots 1870-1936

Father of Dorothy Louise Roots
John Low Roots 1837-1899
Father of Henry Low Roots
Richard Roots 1805-1846
Father of John Low Roots
John Roots 1780-
Father of Richard Roots
Sarah Roots 1801-1893
Daughter of John Roots
John Goodman 1834-1884
Son of Sarah Roots
Charles Ernest Goodman 1862-1921
Son of John Goodman
Jessie Goodman 1898-
Daughter of Charles Ernest Goodman

Tantalising
148. posted 5 Mar 2020, 21:19

A Sarah Low married a Thomas Siers at St Martins in the Fields on 8th May 1825.

On the 27th June 1825, just under two months later, an illegible doc indicates that Sarah Stiers went to the administrators and they completed a form "No 2 for Administrators where there is no leasehold property". Not sure if the value of his estate was less than £100 or his debts were.

If she went to sort out his will on the 27th June 1825, he must have died before that. This means they were married for just over a month.

Why this is tantalising is because I cannot find a death doc for Thomas Siers to confirm anything and because it makes your imagination run wild. How long did she wait after his death before seeing about the will? Or as his widow was she asked to go? Was he dying and did she know he was dying? If so did she marry him for less than £100? (a lot in 1825 I guess) Or did they marry for love when they realised he was dying? Or was it a sudden tragic accident? Or a sudden illness?

Or my preferred one, she married him then killed him....

Corona
149. posted 7 Mar 2020, 21:51

Time for a Brexit moan, been a while. It's happening, nothing I can do about it.

Moan 1 - In the three years + since the referendum, my shopping has gone from £70 a week to a £100 a week and we haven't even left yet.

Moan 2 - We are leaving the EASA, which costs us £1m a year to expand our own agency, the CAA, at a cost of £40m a year. And the airlines will probably have to be part of both. https://www.bbc.co.uk/news/business-51783580

Moan 3 - Report from ONS out today (can't see it on BBC anymore for link, might have been yesterday). saying it has cost us something like £4bn pounds so far. I'm not sure if it was 4 but it was definitely BILLIONS.

Moan 4 - This was earlier in the week, draft US trade deal could increase our economy by 0.12%. However leaving reduces our economy by -7% so net effect is loss of 6.88%. Not to mention the power is with the US in this deal. Taking back control indeed.

To change the subject, back in December, Coronavirus (Covid-19) started in China. It has subsequently spread around the world, most particularly in Iran and Italy. It's a cold that kills 2% of people that get it.

Moan 5 - My Touchstone gig on the 9th May has been cancelled because of Coronavirus. WTF?

Moan 6 - Idiots have been panic buying things like bog roll and pasta. WTF? I understand that you might need to self isolate for 2 weeks so you wouldn't be able to go to shops if you have it but at the same time, poor people can't bulk buy. Sane people won't bulk buy. If the poor and sane people actually need to buy bog roll they can't as it's all sold out.

Not a moan yet.... I am off to Mexico soon for my first holiday since Tenerife last May. It had better not be cancelled because of it. In the summer I'm off to Loreley and that had better not be cancelled as I didn't get ferry crossing insurance for one thing!

and finally... I have had a sniffle all day....!!!!!

Elizabeth Shepherd
150. posted 8 Mar 2020, 18:26

Had some hints for Elizabeth that have resulted in a couple of extensions to the Nicholls/Snelling line:-

John Shepherd -1732
8th great-grandfather
James Shepherd 1721-1767
Son of John Shepherd
Elizabeth Shepherd 1750-1829
Daughter of James Shepherd
Elizabeth Sayer 1771-
Daughter of Elizabeth Shepherd
Thomas Sayer Nicholls 1803-1853
Son of Elizabeth Sayer

Richard Rawlins (if Hannah Smallbone hint correct)
9th great-grandfather
John Rawlins 1705- (no doc confirming Richard & Hannah)
Son of Richard Rawlins
Sarah Rawlins 1727-1770
Daughter of John Rawlins
Elizabeth Shepherd 1750-1829
Daughter of Sarah Rawlins

Went to Sainsburys this morning and whilst the shelves weren't as empty as they might have been, there was toilet roll just not my brand left, there wasn't any rice.

Tescos are acting on it now, restricting essentials:-
https://www.bbc.co.uk/news/business-51790375

In other news, today is our 17th wedding anniversary.

Mary Muscott
151. posted 10 Mar 2020, 14:50

Got a surname for the wife of Joseph Cross that has enabled a new extension to the Pettifer line:-

Samuel Muscot c1690-
8th great-grandfather
Thomas Muscott 1726-
Son of Samuel Muscot
Mary Muscott 1756-
Daughter of Thomas Muscott
Sarah Cross 1796-1879
Daughter of Mary Muscott
Mary Pettifer 1816-
Daughter of Sarah Cross

Mary Smith
152. posted 11 Mar 2020, 22:15

A Mary Smith married William Moses on the 17th January 1803 at St Annes in Soho. With such a common name I know nothing more about her.

However.... A Mary Ann Smith was born c1787 at St George, Middlesex. This might not be her birth name as this is based on a Mary Ann Moses. Mary Ann Moses was in and out of Tower Hamlets Stepney Saint George in the East Workhouse. Her first admission was on the 18th January 1817. She was discharged a month later on the 19th February. Admitted again on the 12th

November 1839. discharged 11th July 1840. Next time was the 2nd October 1840. discharged 3rd April 1841. Then again on the 21st June 1841, 15th September 1843 and 1st April 1841. (no discharge dates for these 3) In 1851 she is on the census as a pauper at this workhouse. Mary Ann Moses died at this workhouse on the 27th October 1866. (not found on 1841 or 1861 census)

A different sort of document was included with the normal admission records which was the 'London, England, Selected Poor Law Removal and Settlement Records 1828-1930'. This 'removal' doc indicates she was with a daughter called Jane who must have been born c1821 but there is nothing to tie Jane to William Moses. This is why I am not convinced that Mary Ann Moses is Mary Smith.

Thomas Inwood
153. posted 11 Mar 2020, 22:56

Predicted relationship: 5th–8th Cousin to sil
Shared DNA: 12cm across 2 segments

Predicted relationship: 5th–8th Cousin to n
Shared DNA: 11cm across 2 segments

DNA Match
5th cousin 1x removed of nephew
William Edwin Payne 1892-1974
Grandfather of DNA Match
Susan Cooper 1858-1929
Mother of William Edwin Payne
Eliza Inwood 1822-
Mother of Susan Cooper
James Inwood 1774-1865
Father of Eliza Inwood
Thomas Inwood 1743-
Father of James Inwood
John Inwood 1776-
Son of Thomas Inwood
Elizabeth Inwood 1817-
Daughter of John Inwood

Alfred Frederick John Martin 1853-1932
Son of Elizabeth Inwood
Florence Louise Martin 1895-1970
Daughter of Alfred Frederick John Martin

Pandemic
154. posted 12 Mar 2020, 20:12

It appears that daughters trip to Paris will be cancelled.

Trump has banned all (Schengen area) European flights going to US.

I am not going to be surprised if our holiday to Mexico will be cancelled but still hopeful as Mexico has no cases yet, it is whether they want our money more than the risk. It's probably more likely our Govt would cancel as it is our PM that has announced all overseas school trips to be cancelled.

Alfredina
155. posted 15 Mar 2020, 20:40

Alfred Jackson and Eleanor/Ellen/Esther Jane Packman had at least 4 children. One of which was Ella Alfredina (Alfreda) Jackson. Ella was born on the 25th April 1891 and baptised on the 3rd June 1891 at Preston Nr Faversham. She married Alfred Long in Southwark in 1912. Ella died on the 18th February 1974, she was living at 9 Hendham Rd, SW17 and left £17,283 in her will.

Obviously the reason for this post was her unusual middle name.

My son is self isolating. He came down with a temperature and cough on Friday night. Truth be told all four of us self isolate the whole time anyway, we are an unsociable family! So I am taking him up drinks and food (though not today, he has added grief of toothache as well), and spraying anything he might have touched when he does leave the room with antibacterial spray. Poor thing is sort of self employed so he will lose money this week having to stay off work.

In more fun news, I went on a Hidden London tour of Moorgate tube station this afternoon. It was quite interesting and cool to be in bits of the Underground that haven't been used for 90 years.

Wraight
156. posted 15 Mar 2020, 20:57

So here is an example of where a common ancestor hint is not quite right and so investigation is required. I only looked at this Wraight because I didn't have James Wraight confirmed and it turns out I still don't have him confirmed. Didn't help that the hint had Mary Pearce instead of Edward Wraight and that Ellen/Eleanor Jane Packham was illegitimate.

5th–8th Cousin to sil no match to nephew
Shared DNA: 6 cM across 1 segments

The hint suggested (with extra incorrect bits in brackets):-

DNA Match
6th cousin 1x removed of nephew
Talbot William Jackson 1893- 1960 (Talbutt)
Grandfather of DNA Match
Eleanor Jane Packman 1864-1897 (Ellen)
Mother of Talbot William Jackson
Caroline Packman 1845-1913
Mother of Eleanor Jane Packman
Harriett Wraight 1810-1890
Mother of Caroline Packman
Edward Wraight 1776-1838 (*Mary Pearce 1781-1867)
Father of Harriett Wraight
James Wraight 1759-1853
Father of Edward Wraight
Celia Wraight 1791-1867
Daughter of James Wraight
George Saddleton 1811-1899
Son of Celia Wraight

However I believe the match is as follows:-

DNA Match
6th cousin 2x removed of nephew
Talbot William Jackson 1893-
Grandfather of DNA Match
Eleanor Jane Packman 1864-1897
Mother of Talbot William Jackson
Caroline Packman 1845-1913
Mother of Eleanor Jane Packman
Harriett Wraight 1810-1890
Mother of Caroline Packman
Edward Wraight 1777-1838
Father of Harriett Wraight
William Wraight 1725-1791
Father of Edward Wraight
James Wraight 1759-1853
Son of William Wraight
Celia Wraight 1791-1867
Daughter of James Wraight

I already had William Wraight matched. Still a worthwhile exercise as Edward Wraight has a story to type up.

The Lovers Manual
157. posted 15 Mar 2020, 21:22

It is not clear who the parents of William Wraight were but he was born c1725. On the 26th April 1750, he married Hannah Goodwin/Gooden in Blean. They had a daughter a year later.

In 1753, William subscribed to "The Lover's Manual. Being a choice collection of poems from the most approv'd modern authors. With several original Poems. In five books, 1753, W., E.. London, Sandwich; Subject: poetry" This subscription also gives his occupation as a 'writing master literature/education'.

The poems presumably worked as William and Hannah had at least 4 more children between 1754 and 1764. Hannah must have died between 1764 and 1777 because William married Lucy Spratt on the 6th April 1777 at Hernhill.

The poems worked on Lucy too, they had at least 6 children before he died in 1791. He was in his sixties when his last son was born. Lovers manual indeed! William was buried in Saltwater, Kent on the 30th January 1791.

Caroline Packman
158. posted 16 Mar 2020, 20:04

Caroline Packman was baptised on the 29th March 1846. She lived with her parents and siblings until at least 1861. In 1864, she had a daughter out of wedlock. Caroline also had a son in 1867 and another daughter in 1870, also out of wedlock.

In 1871, Caroline, Ellen/Eleanor (6), Percy (4) and Mary Ann (1), were all in Faversham Union Workhouse. Unfortunately, I can't locate any admission or discharge papers for them. They must have been discharged by at least 1877 as Caroline had another child, she could have been born in the workhouse however I believe they were out by then.

Henry Branchett was born in 1838 in Faversham. He married an Anne Maria Kent in Faversham in 1855. They lived together until her death in 1872. Not 100% sure about this death date as he has a son, also called Henry, born in 1874.

In 1881, Caroline Packman is living with Henry Branchett and she now has another daughter. She is listed as his 'housekeeper'. In 1882 she has another daughter.

On the 26th April 1886, Caroline married Henry in Faversham. By this time Caroline had 6 children out of wedlock, 3 of which are probably Henrys.

Caroline and Henry had two sons after getting married, Alfred and William. Caroline died in 1913 in Faversham.

Battle of Bossenden Woods
159. posted 16 Mar 2020, 22:19

Edward Wraight was the son of wealthy landowner, William Wraight and his wife Lucy Spratt. He was baptised at Hernhill on the 14th December 1777. He married Mary Pearce at Hernhill on the 29th July 1798. Edward and Mary went on to have at least 11 children between 1799 and 1822.

In the book "The Last Rising of the Agricultural Labourers - Rural Life and protest in Nineteenth Century England " by Barry Reay, Edward and Mary are mentioned several times. They are landowners having a comfortable farmers life but I don't want to quote lots of stuff when I haven't bought the book. They weren't poor is the main point.

On the 29th May 1838, William Courtenay and his followers began a protest that resulted in a constable being killed. The magistrates sent out the 45th Foot, about 100 soldiers to deal with the situation. These 100 soldiers faced 30 or so men armed with nothing more than sticks on the 31st May 1838. The soldiers killed 8 men, one of which was Edward Wraight. More on the 'Battle of Bossenden Woods':-
https://en.wikipedia.org/wiki/Battle_of_Bossenden_Wood

A public hint has this newspaper article about the post mortem:-

"EDWARD WRAIGHT, A RIOTER

Mr. Andrews stated that he found a gun-shot wound upon the deceased; the ball entered at the eighth left rib. There was a second wound at the posterior part of the right scapula, and a bayonet wound in the right axilla. Either of these wounds would have produced death.
Verdict - Justifiable Homicide."

Edward was buried at Hernhill on the 5th June 1838. A description of the funeral can be found on page 141 of Barry Reays book mentioned above.

Cancelled
160. posted 17 Mar 2020, 23:45

Mexico is officially cancelled.

Closed
161. posted 19 Mar 2020, 08:54

Well that's it, schools are closed. The UK is shut! Everyone has to be indoors unless essential to be outside. In 3 weeks I have gone to excitement about holiday being soon to not even being allowed to go to the office.

I feel for the years doing GCSEs and A Levels as exams are cancelled. Though not as much as I feel for the clubs, bars and restaurants and other small businesses that are going to go under. Not as much as I feel for all the workers on zero contracts and temps who have no jobs now. The loan offer from the Govt is pointless, how will they pay it back? What they need is to offer redundancy money that is not a loan for a start.

Sterling lowest in 30 years. Stock markets freefalling.

All this because (UK so far) there have been 2,626 confirmed cases of which 100 have died.

It's because people get a cold and have to self isolate. And because people want a two week skive so say they have a cold to get two weeks of work. We know the vast majority haven't got it because of the 56,221 tests that have been taken on people considered severe enough to be tested, only 4% did. How many people like my son (who is a lot better now but going stir crazy) are there as self isolating stats are not available? Did he have it? Doubtful.

I am trying to take the view that an overreaction causing inconvenience is better than an underreaction causing deaths.

Finally
162. posted 20 Mar 2020, 19:47

Govt has announced bars, cafes, restaurants, nightclubs, theatres, cinemas, gym and leisure centres to close with Govt paying 80% of salary (up to £2,500 a month).

Still need something for self employed that is better than SSP. I think renters (unless self employed) should be ok now Govt is covering their wages.

Mothers Day
163. posted 22 Mar 2020, 23:05

I had booked for daughter and I to go to Sevendroog Castle yesterday for a guided tour and an afternoon tea. That along with seeing Lazuli was obviously cancelled. I went and walked the dog (noticeably more people in the woods) and when I got back I was banned from the kitchen. I hoped they were cooking dinner but it was better than that, they had prepared an afternoon tea in the garden! Was so lovely. Best Mothers Day surprise ever. Sadly they couldn't/wouldn't recreate French prog in the evening.

Today I got hyacinths (bestest smell in the world) and went to McD to get breakfast. It's been Drive Thru/Take Away only with no seating since the restaurant ban. Today they announced they are closing all together! No more Happy Meals or Sausage Bagels for me for a while! Probably a good thing health wise.

Hadn't occurred to me that everyone eats out and get take aways as much as we do. That is a contributing factor for the supermarkets being empty, we are all actually having to cook for ourselves now.

Following the social distancing protocol I did not meet my Mum today. I left her some gifts on her doorstep, got back in car, phoned her to answer door, waved and drove off. I wasn't even sure that was allowed but compared to the other idiots yesterday.... People are going to the Highlands, to Cornwall, the seaside, the parks, the Lake District... Snowdon yesterday reported its highest visitor numbers in living memory. There is so much wrong with this behaviour in a pandemic I don't know where to start. I know I have been saying its an over reaction but I go by the rules made by it. So of course as we can't be trusted to be socially distant I guess it will be the army on the street next to ensure we are.

Lockdown
164. posted 23 Mar 2020, 23:14

Well after the behaviour of some at the weekend, this was expected. 3 weeks, all non essential shops closed, no groups of more than 2 etc. etc.

Clap the NHS
165. posted 26 Mar 2020, 23:01

The self employed are getting same deal as employed people now, that's good.

This evening, (following quite a prolific social media campaign which seemed to spring from nowhere and made me roll my eyes initially), at 8pm, it seemed like the majority of the UK went outside and clapped the NHS staff. Really quite lovely.

Unsurprisingly, the US now has the most positive tests now. Trump responds by saying China are lying about their stats. No, China instigated lockdown pdq and you still haven't.

The Month Everything Changed
166. posted 28 Mar 2020, 08:17

This - from the BBC
https://www.bbc.co.uk/news/stories-52066956 by Jon Kelly

"In the space of a month, the United Kingdom has transformed beyond recognition. And most of us haven't had time to stop and take stock.

One Friday afternoon, when the UK was another country, a chalkboard leaned against the outside wall of a country pub. A message had been written in neat, thin capital letters.

"Unfortunately a customer who visited us has tested positive for the coronavirus," it read. "So as a precautionary measure we are closing for a full deep clean." It was signed by the landlord and landlady, who apologised for the inconvenience.

The pub was located along a quiet, narrow road just outside Haslemere in Surrey. The patient who had gone there lived somewhere in the county. Unlike previous British cases detected up to that point - he was the 20th - he hadn't been abroad recently. As far as anyone knew, he was the first to catch the virus inside the UK.

On the same day, 28 February 2020, came another news update. A grimmer milestone. A British man who'd been infected on the Diamond Princess cruise ship became the first UK citizen to die, in Japan, from Covid-19.

That afternoon, children were still in classrooms and adults were still at work. People shook hands and hugged and kissed. In the evening, they went to pubs and restaurants. Some went on dates and others visited elderly relatives. They assembled in groups and mingled with residents of other households.

As the weekend went on, football fans crammed into stadiums. Worshippers gathered in churches, mosques, temples and synagogues.

You could go outside for as long as you liked, if you didn't mind the rain. On supermarket shelves, toilet paper and paracetamol were plentiful. Recent storms had left large swathes of the country flooded, but for most British people, life went on as it always had and seemingly always would.

Insofar as any of this describes a British way of life, though, it was one that ceased to exist entirely within just a few weeks.

The changes didn't happen smoothly, in steady, barely noticeable steps. Instead, the UK's sense of what was normal shifted in sudden movements, as though a ratchet was being yanked.

On 28 February 2020 people in the UK were already taking notice of the outbreak. It would have been difficult to ignore entirely the headlines about what was happening in China, South Korea, Iran and Italy. The first confirmed cases among travellers returning to the UK had come as early as January, but it still seemed possible to regard this as something happening, for the most part, a long way away.

Not every newspaper front page that Friday morning led with Covid-19 - the Daily Mail splashed on the saga of Harry and Meghan, the Daily Express with Brexit talks - but most did. In the final week of the month 442,675 phone calls were made to the non-emergency NHS line 111. People weren't yet panicking, but a generalised sense of low-level anxiety was everywhere.

By 1 March, the virus had reached the four corners of the United Kingdom - cases had been detected in England, Northern Ireland, Scotland and Wales. Two days later, with the total number at 51, Prime Minister Boris Johnson stood behind a lectern and launched the government's Coronavirus Action Plan. The outbreak was declared a "level four incident".

Up to a fifth of the workforce might be off sick at its peak, the prime minister warned. Schools might have to close and large-scale gatherings be reduced. However seriously anyone took the warning, it was still difficult to visualise.

The following day, a woman in her 70s with an underlying condition - those last four words soon became grimly familiar to anyone who followed news bulletins - became the first person to die inside the UK after testing positive for the virus. The first reports of hand sanitiser selling out in supermarkets were published.

Each day the number of confirmed cases crept up - 115 by 5 March, 206 by 7 March, 273 by 8 March. On 11 March, the day that the World Health Organization declared a pandemic, Liverpool FC hosted Atletico Madrid - who were already playing their home games behind closed doors.

There were anxieties about whether it was a great idea to allow the 3,000 Spanish supporters to fly into a major British city where they would eat, drink, mingle and sleep. Anyone with plans to fly out of the UK was beginning to reconsider.

Another twist of the ratchet was imminent.

The following day, the government's Sage committee of scientific experts was shown revised modelling of the likely death toll. The figures, according to the Sunday Times, were "shattering". If nothing was done, there would be 510,000 deaths. Under the current "mitigation" strategy - to shield the most vulnerable while letting everyone go about their business mostly as normal - there would be a quarter of a million.

Now, it was decided, the strategy was to be one of "suppression". Anyone with a continuous cough or a fever was told to self-isolate. On Friday 13, the London Marathon, the Premier League and English Football League and May's local elections were all postponed. Scotland had its first coronavirus-related death.

Saturday 14 and Sunday 15 March was the last relatively normal weekend. You couldn't watch league football but you could go to the pub. Hand sanitiser now wasn't to be found on any supermarket shelves, but you could tell your friends about your plans to practise "social distancing" if you met them on the street.

Around the country, people looked at Italy, France and Spain, which had already gone into lockdown, and wondered if the UK was next. Volunteers began forming mutual aid groups to deliver food and medicine to vulnerable people who were self-isolating.

In person and on WhatsApp, families and groups of friends argued about what it all meant. The more anxious wondered why the British government was moving more cautiously than its counterparts on the continent. The more blasé complained about why they were going to all this bother. Wasn't it just a bit of flu?

The latter sentiment was exactly the kind of thing the government's advisers were most worried about. On Monday 16, the prime minister advised against "non-essential" travel, urged people to avoid pubs and clubs and work from home.

Across the country, kitchen tables were cleared to make way for laptops. Thanks to Skype and the virtual meetings app, Zoom, white-collar workers started getting a glimpse of their colleagues' interior decor. Those who couldn't do their jobs like this wondered how on Earth they were supposed to earn money and stay safe.

On 17 March, the government began holding daily press conferences - events that would soon become regular viewing for nervous families. Just six days after presenting his budget, the Chancellor, Rishi Sunak, announced £300bn in loan guarantees - a huge expansion of state intervention in the economy by a Conservative government.

But although the UK had been told not to go to restaurants, cafes and pubs, many restaurants, cafes and pubs stayed open. They were quieter than usual but some customers still came. On the evening of Friday 20, the prime minister - who in a long career as a newspaper columnist had steadfastly demonstrated libertarian instincts - ordered restaurants, cafes and pubs to close, a measure that even in the darkest moments of World War Two would have been unthinkable.

For much of the weekend that followed, there was bright sunshine, and people poured outside to take advantage of it - it was one of the last leisure options open to them. But when they crowded into parks and on to the summit of Snowdon they were seen - and widely condemned. This was not how "social distancing" - now regarded as everyone's social duty - was meant to operate.

The lockdown was coming.

On Monday 23, most school pupils - those whose parents weren't designated key workers - didn't go back to their classes. Exams, proms, farewells to classmates and teachers would now never happen.

That night at 20:30, the television screens showed the prime minister sitting behind a desk. He was about to announce some of the most draconian restrictions on individual liberty the UK had ever seen.

You could only leave home to exercise once a day, travel to and from work when absolutely necessary and only go shopping for essential items. You had to stand two metres apart from people you didn't live with. You weren't to gather in public in groups bigger than two.

The British people were being told to avoid human contact when they needed it most.

All through the following week, people would look forward to their one state-sanctioned form of outdoor exercise a day. Or they would stand in front of their laptops, following the instructions set by the fitness coach, Joe Wicks.

By the time the weekend arrived, there were more than 537,000 confirmed cases in 175 countries. More than a quarter of all the people on the planet were living under some kind of restrictions in their social contact and movements.

British life had been transformed so dramatically, and so fast, that you hadn't had time to dwell on it. On 28 February, London's Excel Centre had been hosting The Baby Show, "the UK's largest parenting event". A month later, the venue was a giant field hospital.

This wasn't normal.

Everything was described as "unprecedented" now, because it was. Speaking to the BBC's The World At One, historian Lord Peter Hennessy predicted that, in future, post-war Britain will be demarcated "BC and AC - before corona and after corona".

Before 28 February, the UK was still widely portrayed as a place divided by Brexit, with younger, metropolitan Britons on one side, and their older counterparts in towns and the countryside on the other. That soon came to seem an anachronism. Elderly people were most at risk and those of working age, in the NHS and other key professions, were there to try and save them. Everyone was in this together.

The framing of political debate since 2016 seemed inadequate to the new reality. Coronavirus would not be defeated by a populist attack on the elites. More than ever, the UK needed experts to lead the way. But the experts needed the masses, too - if the vast majority of the population didn't act, then Covid-19 couldn't be stopped.

Initially, the lockdown was supposed to last three weeks. But a month on from 28 February, the UK is settling in for the long haul, with the prime minister, the health secretary and the first in line to the throne all having tested positive for the virus.

You remember your last trip to the gym, the last drink you had in a cafe or a pub, the last time you hugged your mum or your grandad. You think about the life you once took for granted. You wonder if it will ever return."

Million

That's a global milestone reached today. Also 900,000 people have applied for Universal Credit. That's a scary amount of people facing hardship. Eddie Large has died and had tested positive which is first person I have heard of that has died. Sadly for husband, an ex colleague of his died today. Apparently felt unwell, took himself to hospital and never left. How very sad for his family.

James Smith
168. posted 6 Apr 2020, 07:48

Not sure if I already had confirmation of James Smith/Mary Pettifer as I already had a different grandchild of in my tree. As with the other grandchild I can't locate the parents. Daughter and nephew have no matches and my son has a stronger match than me:-

Predicted relationship: 5th–8th Cousin to son
Shared DNA: 12cm across 1 segment

Predicted relationship: 5th–8th Cousin to me
Shared DNA: 8cm across 1 segment

Predicted relationship: 5th–8th Cousin to Mum
Shared DNA: 14cm across 1 segment

DNA Match
4th cousin 1x removed to me
William Edward G Short 1919-1967
Grandfather of DNA Match
Margaret Eva Myrtle Smith 1897-1982
Mother of William Edward G Short
Pettifer James Smith 1847-1918
Father of Margaret Eva Myrtle Smith
James Smith 1814-
Father of Pettifer James Smith
Ann Smith 1836-1897
Daughter of James Smith
Thomas Nicholls 1860-1896

Son of Ann Smith
Florence Catherine M Nicholls 1893-1927
Daughter of Thomas Nicholls

In other news, two weeks lockdown today so entering third week tomorrow. My best friend at school has just come out of self isolation, she sounds like she was very ill. (Also adds to my doubt that boy had it at all, his symptoms were so different.) An old cadet friend of mine who lives in Seattle had to be tested as his wife works for the prison service. He has tested positive although not displaying any symptoms but is understandably concerned. The Marquess of Bath (Longleat) has died with it though he was very old. Boris has been admitted to hospital. His temperature should have gone by now so having checks, doesn't sound like he is on ventilators. Yet.

Tucknott Tree
169. posted 7 Apr 2020, 15:18

SiL and nephew have recently had a match that has made me want to up date Appendix 26. I am still unsure of the connection between them and this match, it is unlikely I will ever know.

Anyway - revised appendix 26. My tree on ancestry goes back another couple of generations but as not 100% sure those ancestors are right, I have not included them.

INDEX

GREEN

John Banks 35
William Banks 99
Thomas Barber 105
Thomas Bourne 75
James Carley 33, 37
Jesse Carley 48
Joseph Cross 33, 36
Henry Freer 9
William Freer 9
John Green 87
Thomas Harris 32
John Lewis 76
John Osbon 39
Thomas Sayer 33
James Smith 168
Timothy Suter 93
William Suter 34, 93
Francis Wilson 13

MADDOX

Robert Alfred Aylen 16
Robert Aylen 130
Thomas Aylen 18
Henry Lewis 110
James Pratt 17
John Stafford 15

PATERSON

Joseph King 48
Greenup Moorsom 134
Alexander Mustart 5, 7, 23, 44, 98
George Robinson 135, 138, 140
Thomas Storm 136
Wilkins 125

PEDIGREES

BRAIN

Jaques Lucas (Luckhurst) 145

GARDNER

Matthew Saggers 131

GREEN

Roger Banks 99
John Bollard 99
Nicholas Butler 99
Henry Freer 9
Thomas Gamble 9
William Ince 99
Samuel Muscott 151
Samuel Parker 8
Richard Rawlins 150
John Shepherd 150

PATERSON

Henry Cowie 2 (*not 100%*)
Alison Crawford 45
John Mustart 45
Johnne Scobie 45
John Taylor 45
John Watson 45

STORIES

BRAIN

Joseph Charles Bentley *Chihuahua* 120
Juarez Stake of Zion 121
Richard Bentley 122
John Valentine Inwood 101
Ella Alfredina Jackson 155
Daniel Luckhurst *French Huguenots* 144
Henry John Packer *Dreadnought Seamans Hospital* 145
Caroline Packman 158
Hailstone Pritty 128
George Wigzell *Kent Cricketer* 146
Edward Wraight *Battle of Bossenden Woods* 159
William Wraight *The Lovers Manual* 157

GARDNER

William Clark 129
Sarah Low 148

GREEN

Charlotte Barber 105
Douglas Byng 141
Charles Costick *Coastguard* 88
Elizabeth Green 86
James Inkerman Green *Navy/Publican* 85
Mary Ann Kirby 11
Urbane Lewis 77
Mary Turfitt 31
Gordon John Wingate *Grenadier Guard* 84

MADDOX

Charles Aylen 112
Mary Hopper 108

PATERSON

Stuart Alexander *Fifth Lord Gartnafueran* 83
Ludovic Colquhoun 98
Jonathan Grindley *HMS St Vincent* 27
Josephine Jessie Marie Grindley 25
Lura Lavinia Grindley 26
Greenup Moorsom(s) 139
Isabella Moorsom 137
Alexander Mustart 44
William Struthers 82
John Wilkins\Tasker 124
Jane Wilkinson 111

www.ingramcontent.com/pod-product-compliance
Lightning Source LLC
Chambersburg PA
CBHW051455250726
48655CB00001B/429